ALSO BY JOEL OSTEEN

The Christmas Spirit
It's Your Time
Hope for Today Bible
Become a Better You
Become a Better You Journal
Daily Readings from Become a Better You
Your Best Life Now
Your Best Life Now for Moms
Your Best Life Now Study Guide
Your Best Life Now Journal
Daily Readings for Your Best Life Now
Your Best Life Begins Each Morning
Scriptures and Meditations for Your Best Life Now
Living Stress Free
Joel Osteen: Living the Joy Filled Life
Starting Your Best Life Now
30 Thoughts for Victorious Living

Daily Readings from

IT'S YOUR TIME

*90 Devotions for Activating
Your Faith, Achieving Your Dreams,
and Increasing in God's Favor*

JOEL OSTEEN

FREE PRESS
New York London Toronto Sydney

Free Press
A Division of Simon & Schuster, Inc.
1230 Avenue of the Americas
New York, NY 10020

First Free Press hardcover edition December 2010

FREE PRESS and colophon are trademarks of Simon & Schuster, Inc.

For information about special discounts for bulk purchases,
please contact Simon & Schuster Special Sales at 1-866-506-1949
or business@simonandschuster.com.

The Simon & Schuster Speakers Bureau can bring authors to your live event.
For more information or to book an event contact
the Simon & Schuster Speakers Bureau at
1-866-248-3049 or visit our website at www.simonspeakers.com.

Manufactured in the United States of America

1   3   5   7   9   10   8   6   4   2

ISBN 978-1-4516-0987-5
ISBN 978-1-4516-1039-0 (ebook)

CONTENTS

INTRODUCTION

I WROTE *IT'S YOUR TIME* to speak faith into the lives of others, to encourage them during tough times, to call forth seeds of greatness planted by God, and to assure them that their best days lie ahead. This *Daily Readings for It's Your Time* is a ninety-day devotional with excerpts from the original book designed to emphasize those same messages. Like *It's Your Time*, this devotional based upon it is divided into five main sections. Each is designed to build on the other. The goal is not simply to inspire and motivate you, but also to help you see that God's plan is at work in your life.

This devotional is not meant to be an exhaustive treatment of any particular passage of Scripture, but instead is intended to encourage you to immerse yourself in His word and inspire a wholehearted love of God. And the suggested prayer at the end of each day's entry is simply a place to begin your communication with your Heavenly Father. The book begins with a section entitled "It's Time to Believe," because tough times require strong faith, because this too will pass. "It's Time for Favor" is the section about faith fortification. In "It's Time for Restoration," I offer tools of forgiveness and renewal. "It's Time to Trust" builds your resolve by reminding you of those things you can trust: that all things work together for good. Finally, I've concluded the book with "It's

Time to Stretch," which will motivate you to step into your divine destiny.

Each of the daily readings was selected to emphasize one of those five keys. I've added other features for each to help you apply and live out God's truth:

- Scripture Readings to *It's Your Time*
- Key Bible verses
- Today's Prayer to *It's Your Time*
- Today's Thought to *It's Your Time*

These ninety readings should be read at a one-each-day pace so that they carry you through three months or so. I'm convinced that by the end of that period, you will come to see that it truly is your time for healing and advancement. As you read this devotional day to day, keep your heart pure, strive for excellence, and prepare yourself, because it's your time for God's goodness, favor, and restoration. It's your time to walk in the fullness of His blessing!

—Joel Osteen

PART ONE

IT'S TIME TO BELIEVE

GOD IS ON YOUR SIDE

DAILY READING 1:1

SCRIPTURE READING TO *IT'S YOUR TIME*   GALATIANS 6

*So let's not allow ourselves to get fatigued doing good.
At the right time we will harvest a good crop if we don't
give up, or quit.*

                       GALATIANS 6:9 (THE MESSAGE)

WHILE ON VACATION IN COLORADO, I woke up early for a hike. The three-mile trail ran to the peak of Beaver Creek Mountain. At the base a sign said it should take about three hours to reach the top. Looking up to my destination, I was intimidated. The trail was extremely steep. The altitude at the base was about 8,000 feet above sea level. The peak stood at more than 11,000 feet.

Just walking up the first set of stairs I began breathing heavier than normal. I had to remind myself to take it easy. At home in Houston, I run several miles a few times a week and play a lot of basketball. But the elevation there is only 50 feet above sea level. The thinner air in Colorado had me doubting whether I could make it to the top.

I started out with just my cell phone and a bottle of water. Determined, I set a pretty good pace. The first fifteen minutes seemed fairly easy. The next fifteen minutes were increasingly difficult. I felt as though I were carrying an extra load. I had to stop every so often to catch my breath.

About forty-five minutes into my hike, the trail got extremely steep—almost like I was climbing straight up. My pathway snaked skyward through thick stands of aspen and ponderosa pine. The view was both beautiful and daunting. Despite being in shape, my legs were burning and my chest was pounding.

As I climbed over a big ridge, I had to stop for air. Sweat was pouring off my body. I thought, *If there's another two hours like this, I don't know if I can make it.*

Up to that point, I had not seen anyone else on the path. Suddenly, an older gentleman heading down the mountain came around a curve. He wore a T-shirt, shorts, and hiking shoes and carried a walking stick. He seemed cool and calm. And he read me pretty well. As we passed, he said something that changed my whole perspective. He smiled kindly and said in a calm voice, "You are closer than you think."

Hearing those words, I felt rejuvenated, as if he'd breathed new life into my lungs. Energy surged through my body. My legs grew stronger. I caught a second wind. From that point forward, with every stride, I repeated those words of encouragement: "I will make it. I'm closer than I think."

God has put dreams and desires in every person's heart. We all have goals we want to accomplish and situations we believe will be turned around. Sometimes it seems to take longer than we thought. Sometimes things don't work out the way we planned, and it's easy to lose enthusiasm. Negative thoughts come to us that say, "It's never going to change." If we're not careful, we'll get discouraged and end up just settling where we are.

Don't let that be you today! Don't give up just because things seem hard. You are closer than you think! You've invested so much and you never know, just another few days of believing, another few weeks of doing the right thing, another few months of staying in faith, and you could see that situation turn around. Remember, God is on your side!

✤ Today's Prayer to *It's Your Time* ✤

Father God, today I come to You again, believing that You are working behind the scenes on my behalf. Give me Your strength to keep moving forward into the place of victory You have for me. In Jesus' Name. Amen.

✤ Today's Thought to *It's Your Time* ✤

I must keep standing and keep believing because I am closer than I think to fulfilling every desire He's placed inside of me!

TODAY IS THE DAY!

DAILY READING 1:2

Scripture Reading to *It's Your Time*   Habakkuk 2

> *This vision is for a future time.*
> *It describes the end, and it will be fulfilled.*
> *If it seems slow in coming, wait patiently,*
> *for it will surely take place.*
> *It will not be delayed.*
>
> Habakkuk 2:3 (NLT)

Down in the Florida Keys, there was a treasure hunter whose motto was "Today's the day." Every day for sixteen years, Mel Fisher sent his divers out with those encouraging words to find a Spanish ship that sank off the Keys in 1622. He often had to pay his men in promises while dodging bill collectors. He and his family lived on a leaky houseboat for years. One of his sons, a daughter-in-law, and a diver were lost at sea as they searched for the treasure.

Still, Fisher never gave up. He refused to abandon his dream or to give in to critics and doubters. He held on by declaring that each day would be *the* day. Then, in 1985, Mel's divers found "the Mother lode" of gold and silver and jewelry from the wreckage of the Spanish galleon. Nearly thirty years later, divers were still bringing up treasure from that site.

Is today the day for you to accomplish your goal, to land your dream job, to find love, to restore your health? You are closer than you think to a better life, a richer relationship, a healthier body.

Rewards await you if you stay steadfast in your faith.

Don't let doubters ruin your optimistic spirit. If somebody says to you, "What is it with you? What makes you think everything will work out? Do you really believe you will always succeed?" just tell the doubters, "I don't think it will happen. I *know* it will happen! I'm a prisoner of hope. I can't get away from it. I just can't make myself get negative. I just can't make myself complain. Hope feeds my faith and lifts my spirits."

The doubters may say, "Well, I don't know why. I saw the medical report. It doesn't look good for you."

"Yes, but I have another report," you can tell them. "It says God is restoring health back unto me."

"Well, I saw your child. I don't think he'll ever do what's right."

"Really? I have another report. It says as for me and my house, we will serve the Lord."

You may not see any of this in the natural world. It may not look like it will come to pass. But that's okay. The Scripture says, "We walk by faith and not by sight." That means we don't have to see it to believe it. It's just the opposite. If we believe it, *then* we see it.

Take your dreams and the promises God has put in your heart and every day declare that they will come to pass. Just say something like, "Father, I want to thank You that my payday is coming. You said no good thing will You withhold because I walk uprightly. And I believe even right now You are arranging things in my favor."

Are you a prisoner of fear? Worry? Self-pity? Negativity?

Break those chains and become a prisoner of hope. Expect God's favor. Believe that He is working in your life, even right now.

God has put dreams and desires in your heart. We all have goals we want to accomplish and situations we believe we will turn around. But often when it's taking a long time and things are not working out, it's easy to lose our enthusiasm. That's when the negative thoughts come, saying:

It never will change.

You never will get well.

You never will climb out of debt.

That child never will straighten up.

If you listen to those negative thoughts, you will likely become discouraged and give up on your dreams. Many times we miss out on God's best because we give up too soon. We don't realize how close we are to victory.

Hold on to your faith. Another few days of believing, another few weeks of doing the right thing, or another few months of staying in faith and you will see that promise come to pass.

Right now, you are so close to seeing that situation turn around. That answer you've been praying about is just right around the corner. You can't afford to get discouraged. You can't afford to give up now.

That's what the scripture says in Hebrews 10:35. It tells us not to cast away our confidence, for it will be richly rewarded. That's saying if we will stay in faith, if we will keep believing, keep hoping, keep doing the right thing, God promises there will be a reward.

One translation says, in effect, "Don't get discouraged. Payday is coming."

When you're tempted to get down and things are not going your way, you need to keep telling yourself, "This may be hard. It may be taking a long time. But I know God is a faithful God. And I will believe, knowing that my payday is on its way."

Whenever life grows difficult, and the pressure is turned up, that's a sign that your time is near. When lies bombard your mind, when you are most tempted to get discouraged, and when you feel like throwing in the towel, that's not the time to give up. That's not the time to back down. That's the time to dig in your heels. Put on a new attitude. You are closer than you think.

You may have had a lot of things come against you. I know

sometimes it seems like the more you pray, the worse it gets. You do the right thing but get the wrong results. Maybe you're treating somebody kindly and respectfully, but they're being unkind and discourteous to you. The easy thing would be to say, "Forget it. I don't have to put up with this"; "This marriage never will work"; "I'll never be able to raise this child"; or "I don't like this job."

Instead of getting discouraged, instead of going around all sour, you need to have the attitude to say, "I've come too far to stop now. I've been through too much to back down. I realize the pressure has been turned up because I'm about to give birth to my dreams!"

✺ Today's Prayer to *It's Your Time* ✺

Heavenly Father, thank You for the destiny that You have deposited into my heart. I choose to stand in faith knowing that You are working behind the scenes. Give me strength and wisdom to follow You so I can embrace all You have for me.

✺ Today's Thought to *It's Your Time* ✺

The depth of my past is an indication of the height of my future. It's my time to step out and embrace all that God has for me!

MAINTAIN AN OPTIMISTIC ATTITUDE

DAILY READING 1:3

Scripture Reading to *It's Your Time*   Leviticus 26:1–13

> *I will give you rain in due season, and the land shall yield
> her increase and the trees of the field yield their fruit.*
> Leviticus 26:4 (AMP)

My wife, Victoria, once lost a ring her mother had given her. It was a diamond band that had been in the family for several generations. Although it was valuable, it held even more sentimental value to us. Sometimes when we'd go on trips, Victoria hid the ring in our house. We thought maybe she'd hidden it and forgotten the hiding place. So we looked, and looked, and looked in every drawer, in every cabinet. I looked behind couches and between cushions. I found things that I hadn't seen in ten years. But never Victoria's ring.

After a couple of months of looking on and off, I finally gave up. That ring was nowhere to be found. But every few days, I heard Victoria pray: "Father, thank You that I will find my ring. Thank You, for You are leading me and guiding me."

I didn't say anything out loud, but inside, being the great man of faith that I am, I thought, *Victoria, you are wasting your time. We have turned this house upside down. That ring is just not here.*

It's funny, but when my mother-in-law noticed that Victoria was not wearing the ring and asked her about it, she said, "Oh, Mom. I've put it away in a really safe place."

I thought, *Yeah, so safe that we can't even find it.*

As the months went by, I probably heard Victoria say she would find that ring five hundred times. I never once heard her give up and say, "It's gone. I've lost it. What will I do?"

She had an optimistic attitude. "I'm closer than I think. I know any day that ring will show up."

Three years later we were driving home from Victoria, Texas, two hours south of Houston. We had just ministered for my brother-in-law Jim and my sister Tamara. Driving on the freeway, eleven at night, Victoria said, "Joel, you'd better slow down. You will get a ticket."

"I won't get a ticket," I said. "We're only going seventy. The speed limit is sixty-five."

"No, the speed limit is sixty at night," Victoria said.

"No, it's sixty-five."

"Joel, I'm telling you, you need to slow down."

I laughed. "Victoria, I have the favor of God."

God has such a sense of humor. Just about that time, I looked in my rearview mirror and saw the red flashing lights. Then I looked at Victoria and said, "You made me get this ticket."

The officer was a real nice, polite young man. He said, "I need to see your driver's license." I gave it to him.

"Are you the minister?" he asked.

"I am."

"Did you speak at Faith Family Church tonight?"

"I did. In fact, that's my sister's church."

"I know," the officer said. "My father was there. He's the head usher."

"Oh, man. That's great. He was so nice to me."

The officer laughed, but he still asked for my insurance card.

And so Victoria dug deeper and deeper in the glove compartment. It was dark and we were a little uptight about being pulled over. She found every card except the right one.

Finally, with the officer waiting, Victoria took out all the contents of the glove compartment in search of the insurance card. She reached way back inside as far as she could. There, deep down in the darkness, she felt something with a hard, sharp edge. She dug a little deeper, grabbed it, and pulled it out.

Lo and behold, it was her missing ring. She was so excited. She forgot all about looking for the insurance card!

I thought, *Girl, you're rejoicing, and I'm about to go to jail.* "Victoria, that's great. But we still have to find the insurance card," I reminded her.

She finally dug out that, too, and gave it to the officer.

"Joel, I'll let you go," he said. "But first, I have one request. When I come visit your church, will you save me a seat?"

"Officer," I told him, "I'll save you a whole section."

I drove off that night thinking, *God, You are so good. I didn't get a ticket and Victoria found her ring.*

God works in mysterious ways. I thought later that He caused Victoria to find her ring at my expense. But the truth is that Victoria stayed in faith. She had that attitude: "I'm closer than I think."

⚘ Today's Prayer to *It's Your Time* ⚘

Father, I worship You today. I thank You for preparing me for the blessing and promotion You have in my future. I surrender my heart, mind, will, and emotions to You so that I can live as a testimony of Your work in my life.

⚘ Today's Thought to *It's Your Time* ⚘

Right now the Creator of the universe is lining up things in my favor: the right people, the right breaks, the right opportunities.

THE TIDE IS TURNING

DAILY READING 1:4

SCRIPTURE READING TO *IT'S YOUR TIME*   ZECHARIAH 9

> *Come back to the place of safety,*
> *all you prisoners who still have hope!*
> *I promise this very day that I will repay*
> *two blessings for each of your troubles.*
> ZECHARIAH 9:12 (NLT)

A FRIEND TOLD ME A story about an executive who had an interesting print hanging in his office. It depicted a large rowboat stranded on a beach. Two oars rested gently in the sand, with the ocean at low tide twenty or thirty feet behind it. The boat looked too heavy to drag, too big to move. It was just stuck there in the sand.

The picture wasn't a thing of beauty. It wasn't inspiring. In fact, it was depressing. Here was this boat created for the water, a very nice boat made to dance on top of the ocean waves, stuck in the sand.

But at the very bottom of the picture was a small caption that gave meaning to the otherwise unremarkable picture. It read, "The tide always comes back."

With that simple caption, the print took on new meaning: When the tide returned, that stranded boat once again would find its purpose. It would return to the place it was meant to be.

My friend told me that the executive once had gone through a great disappointment. He didn't think he would ever be happy again. Then he saw the painting at a small antiques store and bought it for just a few dollars. Every time he looked at it, he said to himself, "The tide is coming back."

That print spoke faith into his heart. The caption gave him hope that things would change in his favor.

You may find yourself in a similar situation. Stuck. Stranded. Robbed of your purpose. Things may not be going your way. You've lost your energy and enthusiasm.

Heed those words: "The tide is coming back."

Hear my message: God is breathing new life into your dreams.

You will feel the wind of His spirit lift your sails once again. You are not meant to simply endure life. Barely getting by is not acceptable. You were meant to dance on top of the waves.

Remember that it is always darkest before the dawn. More challenges mean you're closer to your victory. Don't give up on your dream. Don't give up your relationship because the waters get rough. Don't give up on living a healthy life because illness brings you down. Times may grow tough, but remember there are rewards for staying in faith.

Today's Prayer to *It's Your Time*

Father, help me to be a prisoner of hope, to get up every day expecting Your favor.

Today's Thought to *It's Your Time*

The tide is coming back. I am closer than I think!

JUMP-START YOUR FAITH

DAILY READING 1:5

SCRIPTURE READING TO *IT'S YOUR TIME*   GALATIANS 6

Don't be misled—you cannot mock the justice of God.
You will always harvest what you plant.
                                    GALATIANS 6:7 (NLT)

BRENDA EHEART CREATED A PLACE that has benefited the lives of many people, young and old. But she would never have gotten the job done if she hadn't relentlessly pursued her dream. This sociology professor has a passion for "unadoptable" children in foster care, kids who rarely know a loving, stable home. They often bounce from one foster home to another. Many have been abused or neglected.

Most age out of the system at eighteen. Often they wind up homeless, on drugs, committing crimes, or in prison. This problem has existed for decades. Professor Eheart wanted to do something about it.

She dreamed of a place where foster care kids would be permanently adopted and cared for by loving parents. These parents would be supported by child therapists, psychologists, and seniors serving as volunteer grandparents.

This professor had no money and no influence. She was told it was too expensive, that the problem was too big.

She did not give up. One day, she learned that an old air force base near her home in Illinois was shutting down. This base had a nice neighborhood of townhomes for air force officers and their families.

Professor Eheart knew nothing about politics. She had no clout. But she convinced the state to give her a million dollars. She bought an entire neighborhood on the old base.

She called it Hope Meadows.

Since it opened in 1994, Hope Meadows has taken nearly one hundred children out of foster care and given them permanent, loving homes. Some have gone on to college and earned degrees. Others have become hardworking, churchgoing members of their communities.

Brenda Eheart and her nonprofit organization recently received a grant so she can create other Hope Meadows around the country. Her once-impossible dream continues to grow.

Sometimes you just need something spoken over your life. You need someone to jump-start your faith, to breathe new life into your dreams. You may have been through a thousand disappointments. In the natural, you may have every reason to give up on what God's put in your heart. But I'm asking you to let this simple phrase take root: *My time is coming.*

God is in control of your life. He knows exactly where you are. He knows even the hidden dreams He has put in you. The Scripture calls these *the secret petitions of our heart.* These are the dreams you have not shared with anyone. Maybe you thought they would never work out, or you buried them because they didn't happen on your timetable.

But God still has a way to bring them to pass. Draw the line in the sand and say, "That's it. I'm done being complacent. I'm done settling for mediocrity. I believe every dream, every promise, even the secret petitions of my heart will come to fulfillment."

When you have that kind of attitude, all the forces of darkness cannot stop God from bringing your dreams to pass.

You may be discouraged. Negative thoughts may come, telling you, *It never will happen. You never will marry. You never will be free of debt. You never will find happiness. This is as good as it gets.*

You have to shake off those thoughts. Say, "Father, You said the path of the righteous gets brighter and brighter. You said no good thing will You withhold because I walk uprightly. You said because I delight myself in You, You would give me the secret petitions of my heart. So Father, I want to thank You that You are in control of my life, good things are in store, and I believe my time is coming."

You will go through unfair situations. We all do. When somebody does you wrong or you get some bad breaks, don't make the mistake of constantly dwelling on the downside. Too many pitch their tents in the land of self-pity. Somebody mistreated them a year ago, five years ago, thirty years ago, and they allow it to poison their lives.

If somebody does you wrong, instead of getting negative and bitter, your attitude should be, *They just did me a favor. They just qualified me for double. And I believe my time is coming. I will come out with twice the joy, twice the peace, twice the victory.*

That's an attitude of hope, an attitude that says, *I will not be defeated. It may look impossible, but I know God can do the impossible. They may have treated me wrong. I'm not worried. I know God is my vindicator. It may be taking a long time, but in due season I know I will reap if I just don't give up.*

You may have been through a series of losses. Life may not seem fair. It's easy to think, *It never will be better. This just is my lot in life.* If you are not careful, your negative thoughts will draw in more of the negative. It begins with one unfair situation, and then we perpetuate it by having and holding on to the wrong mindsets. I'm asking you to break out of that rut. You may have been through unfair situations, but it's not over until God says it's over.

God always has the final say. He is a God of justice. God sees every wrong that's ever been done to you. He sees every unfair situation. He says that if you will stay in faith, if you'll keep your hopes up, He will make your wrongs right. He will bring justice into your life.

Your attitude should be, *It may have been unfair. They may have done me wrong. But I refuse to get bitter. I know my time is coming.*

❧ Today's Prayer to *It's Your Time* ❧

Father in heaven, I ask You to search my heart. Help me, by Your Spirit, to plant good seeds for my future. Use me for Your glory.

❧ Today's Thought to *It's Your Time* ❧

As I stay obedient to the Word of God, I will see those seeds grow. I will rise up higher and enjoy the harvest of blessing God has promised me.

GOD'S PROMISE IS IN YOU

SCRIPTURE READING TO *IT'S YOUR TIME*   LUKE 2

*At that time there was a man in Jerusalem named Simeon.
He was righteous and devout and was eagerly waiting for
the Messiah to come and rescue Israel. The Holy Spirit
was upon him and had revealed to him that he would not
die until he had seen the Lord's Messiah.*

LUKE 2:25–26 (NLT)

IN THE SCRIPTURE GOD TELLS Simeon he would not die until he
saw Christ. Simeon did not understand, but he let God's promise
take root deep down inside. He didn't tell anybody about God's
message. It was just between him and God.

Some commentaries say Simeon waited nearly twenty years. I
can imagine the older he grew, the more he was tempted to think, *I
must not have heard God right. It never will happen. It's been five
years, now ten years.*

No, Simeon had to do just what I'm asking us to do. When those
negative thoughts came, he had to shake it off and say, "No, my
time is coming. The promise is in me. God put it in my heart. And
I will not go to my grave until I see it fulfilled."

He rose every morning hoping, believing, expecting. And God

is faithful, for some twenty years later, Simeon saw that promise come to pass.

God speaks to us all just as he did to Simeon. Deep down on the inside you have dreams that you know will come to pass before you leave this earth. It may be a promise that a child will return to the right path. Maybe your child has been off that path for five, ten, fifteen years.

Do what Simeon did. Just remind God "You put this promise in me that as for me and my house we will serve the Lord. And I believe I will not go to my grave until I see my whole family serving you."

Maybe God put a promise on you that day you were married. You've been through some disappointments, some broken relationships. You're a little older. You're tempted to think it will not happen. No, God has already picked out the right person. And you're never too old.

Just recently I met a couple in their nineties. They'd just had their wedding and were on their honeymoon. Now, I know you don't want to wait until your nineties to get married. I'm just giving you the worst-case scenario. Then again, I heard about this eighty-five-year-old woman who went on a blind date with a ninety-two-year-old man.

She came home very frustrated. Her daughter said, "Mom, what went wrong on your date?"

"I had to slap him three times," she said.

"You mean he tried to get fresh?" the daughter asked.

"No. I thought he was dead."

Maybe God's put one of these promises in you instead: that one day you will write a book, be in management, open a successful business, or join the ministry. But now, like Simeon, you are doubtful that your dream will ever happen. Negative thoughts creep in: *You're getting too old. You don't have the right connections. You've made too many mistakes.*

Sometimes the more we believe, the more we pray, the less likely it looks. It's easy to get complacent and to let the seed die stillborn. But I'm asking you to do what Simeon did.

No matter how long it's been, no matter how tempted you are to get discouraged, get up every morning and just declare it by faith: "My time is coming. The promise is in me, and I will not die until I see it come to pass."

If Simeon were standing before us today, he'd say, "Don't give up on that promise. Your time is coming."

You need to let Simeon's story sink deep down on the inside. Some of you thought it was over. Some of you thought you made too many mistakes. You thought you were getting too old. But it's never too late. God says, essentially, "This is your season. Keep your faith stirred up."

God put a promise in Moses that he would deliver the people of Israel, but Moses made a major mistake. He killed somebody and had to run for his life. Forty years went by. It looked like he was done. It seemed like it was over.

But God never aborts a dream. We may give up on it. We may delay it. But the seed God put in you never dies.

My advice is to stay faithful. Your time is coming.

Maybe you've been working in the same job for twenty years, showing up early, giving it your best, but the promotion has never come.

Do not get bitter. Don't get negative. You're not working unto man. You're working unto God. And if you'll keep the right attitude, your time of promotion will come.

God is keeping the records. He sees every seed you've ever sown. *What you sow you will reap.* If Simeon were standing before us today, he'd say, "Don't give up on that promise. Your time is coming."

❧ Today's Prayer to *It's Your Time* ❧

Father, You put this promise in me to serve You. And I believe I will not go to my grave until I see my whole family serving you.

❧ Today's Thought to *It's Your Time* ❧

I will keep my faith stirred up.

FAN THE FLAME

DAILY READING 1:7

SCRIPTURE READING TO *IT'S YOUR TIME*   II TIMOTHY I

> *For this reason I remind you to fan into flame the gift of*
> *God, which is in you . . .*
>
>   II TIMOTHY 1:6 (NIV)

DR. SYED NAQVI WAS JOGGING on a treadmill in his home when he went into cardiac arrest. Emergency workers and doctors kept the fifty-six-year-old neurologist alive, but he was in a vegetative state, unable to breathe on his own.

His wife, Nina, refused to give up. She contacted another neurologist, a family friend, and pleaded for his help. This doctor had just learned of a new "cooling treatment" for cardiac arrest patients. If the treatment begins within six hours of the attack, the patient has a much greater chance of full recovery.

Dr. Naqvi's brainwaves were nearly flat. They literally put him on ice. His body was cooled for twenty-four hours. His temperature dropped to eight degrees below normal. His wife and other family members waited and prayed.

Was it their time to believe?

Yes, it was.

Five days later, Dr. Naqvi came out of his coma. At first, he was confused and had memory lapses. But within six weeks, his mental functions were fully restored. He went from a life-threatening vegetative state to once again treating his own patients!

Stay in faith. Be a prisoner of hope. God will put the right people in your path. God will bring to fulfillment even the secret petitions of your heart. You must rise up, like Mrs. Naqvi, block out negative thoughts, and say, "You know what? This is for me. With my faith I will ignite this moment. With my faith I will bring forth the dream on the inside."

The Scripture encourages us to fan the flame. At eighty years of age, Moses saw his time come. After thirteen years of being done wrong, Joseph saw his time come. If God did it for them, He can do it for you. Keep your faith stirred up. You've served others. You've given generously. You've sacrificed your time. And that's great. That's what life is all about.

Today's Prayer to *It's Your Time*

Father, I come to You today giving You my disappointments, setbacks, hurts, and broken dreams. I ask that You restore my passion and vision for the future. Let Your flame burn brightly in me now and forevermore.

Today's Thought to *It's Your Time*

I will never let "good enough" be good enough.

GOD HAS MOMENTS OF FAVOR FOR YOU

DAILY READING 1:8

Scripture Reading to *It's Your Time*   Psalm 31

Rescue me from my enemies, Lord; I run to you to hide me.

Psalm 31:15 (NLT)

Marie worked at a small restaurant near Los Angeles. She waited on tables, cooked, cleaned, basically did it all. One day her boss, the owner, said that more and more customers were requesting desserts. At that time the restaurant didn't offer any. The boss told Marie she had to come in earlier to make desserts every morning.

Her first reaction was frustration.

I already work hard enough, she thought. *This is not fair.*

But instead of getting bitter, Marie decided to accept the new duty as a challenge. She set her sights on creating the best desserts she possibly could.

Marie's pies caught on. Customers loved them. In fact, people came to the restaurant just to have a piece of her pie. Her pies became so popular that Marie decided to open her own pie company.

She took a step of faith and things quickly fell into place. She found a bakery. She bought the equipment she needed. It was a moment of favor.

Before long, her little business began to grow and her son joined her. They opened more and more locations. Eventually, Marie Callender's company had 110 restaurants and an entire line of frozen pies and entrees sold in supermarkets!

It doesn't matter where you are right now; God has moments of favor for you, too. You may not be able to figure it out, but that's okay. That's not your job. Your job is to believe. God's already figured it out.

You might say, "Joel, I'm just not that talented."

Can you make a pie? Look what happened to Marie!

I want you to have a bigger vision for your life. There are exciting things in your future. The right people are out there. The breaks you need have already been lined up by the Creator of the universe.

What can stop them? Not the enemy, not other people, nobody can keep you from your destiny—except you.

You may have suffered some bad breaks. You may have tried and failed. Now you may be sitting on the sidelines of life, not expecting anything good. Shake off that defeated mentality. Rise up and say, "This is a new day. It may not have happened in the past, but it will happen someday. I know God has moments of favor coming my way!"

God has already prearranged times of increase, times of blessing. You will have opportunities to meet the right people, opportunities to advance in your career, opportunities to fulfill your dreams. You may not be experiencing any good breaks right now. Maybe you're stuck in a rut. But let me encourage you with this: In your future there are God-ordained moments. He has them planned out for you.

Too many people miss these moments. They tried and failed before, so they quit believing. Or they're distracted. There is so much clutter in their lives, they can't hear the still, small voice inside telling them, *It's your moment of favor!*

We have to be sensitive to God's timing. We may go five years with nothing big happening, and then all of a sudden, a God-ordained moment comes along: You meet someone who changes your life, you get a loan to buy the house of your dreams, you are promoted to a new job.

In a split second you are thrust years ahead.

I can look back over my own life and see the moments that altered my destiny, moments that propelled me to a higher level. When I was in my early twenties, I walked into a jewelry store to buy a battery for my watch. That's where I met Victoria—a moment of favor!

That wasn't a lucky break. That was God bringing time and chance together. He ordained that moment before the foundation of the world. That's why we don't have to worry. We don't have to go around frustrated because things aren't happening as fast as we would like. All we have to do is stay in faith, knowing that God is directing our steps. As long as we keep believing, our moments of favor are on their way.

I love what David said in Psalm 31:15: "God, my times are in Your hands . . ." He was saying, "God, I already know You have supernatural breaks planned out for me. You have the right people, the right opportunities, so I will not be stressed out. I will stay in peace knowing that You will get me to my final destination."

It's easy to get frustrated when your dreams aren't coming to pass on your timetable. But be patient. Prepare yourself. Stay open for signs of opportunity.

Sure, we would love to always be moving ahead with our lives, but we can use the other times to get ready, to sharpen our skills, to deepen our knowledge, to prepare ourselves for promotion.

❧ Today's Prayer to *It's Your Time* ❧

Father, I know You have moments of favor coming my way.

❧ Today's Thought to *It's Your Time* ❧

I will remain alert for signs of opportunity.

GOD IS WAY AHEAD OF YOU

DAILY READING 1:9

SCRIPTURE READING TO *IT'S YOUR TIME*   PROVERBS 24

For though a righteous man falls seven times, he rises again, . . .

PROVERBS 24:16 (NIV)

SAMUEL HERSCHBERGER WAS JUST THREE days away from his tenth birthday when he was in a terrible farm accident. The boy's shirtsleeve was snared in a grinder attached to a tractor. His father, Oba, sprinted to help Samuel, but the sight of his mangled boy caused him to stop and turn away in shock. He was certain that Samuel was dead. He could not look.

Then he heard a tiny, pleading voice. "Dad, please help me."

No one thought Samuel would survive. Eleven doctors worked eighteen straight hours to save him. As you might imagine, the medical costs were staggering for the family. Fellow church members pitched in. But they could barely make a dent.

Still, God had a solution.

The Herschbergers began hosting farm-style dinners in their home to raise money. A Chicago newspaper reported on their fundraising efforts. A few weeks later, Oba had to ask people to stop sending money. "We have so much coming in we can't count it all," he said.

They filled their bathtubs with checks and cash sent by strangers. Many thousands were donated—enough to pay for the thirty-seven operations Samuel has had to endure. Today, he is a fun-loving young man who works on a farm helping raise champion draft horses. His grateful family still welcomes guests for their country dinners.

God knows the end from the beginning. He has solutions to problems you haven't even had.

God may have spoken to someone twenty years ago about that situation you're dealing with right now. He has already marked your moments for mercy. He has marked moments of favor for restoration. He knows how to get you back on the right track.

So go ahead and get your hopes up. Believe that no matter what you have or haven't done, your best days are still out in front of you.

Little things and big things, God has already lined up your moments of favor. Why don't you quit worrying about it? Why don't you stop losing sleep over it? God has you in the palm of His hand. God is aware of all you are facing now and all you will deal with in the future.

The good news is that He already has answers to those problems. The Scripture says, "For I know the plans I have for you," says the Lord. "Plans to prosper you, plans to bless you, plans to give you hope and a future." One verse says, "God has prearranged for you to live the good life."

For every setback, God has prearranged a comeback. For every failure, God has prearranged mercy. For every disappointment, God has prearranged restoration. For every unfair thing, God has prearranged vindication.

We all face disappointments and setbacks. Maybe you got some bad news concerning your health, or maybe a relationship didn't work out. That was a setback. It's easy to get discouraged, lose your enthusiasm, or even be tempted to just settle where you are. But if we're going to see God's best, when you get knocked down, you don't stay down. You get back up again. You have to know that every time adversity comes against you, it's a setup for a comeback!

There is no challenge too difficult, no obstacle too high, no sickness, no disappointment, no person, nothing that can keep you from your God-given destiny. If you stay in faith and keep a good attitude, you will rise again. God will turn those stumbling blocks into stepping-stones, and you'll move forward into the victory He has in store for you!

❧ Today's Prayer to *It's Your Time* ❧

Father in heaven, thank You for setting me up for success in everything I do. I choose to trust and rely on You knowing that Your plans are for my good. I know my best days are ahead of me and I look forward to the blessings You have in store for me.

❧ Today's Thought to *It's Your Time* ❧

God knows the end from the beginning and He had the solutions before I had the problems.

THE WINDS OF GOD'S FAVOR

DAILY READING 1:10

SCRIPTURE READING TO *IT'S YOUR TIME*   ACTS 2:1–13

And suddenly there came a sound from heaven as of a rushing mighty wind, and it filled all the house where they were sitting.

ACTS 2:2 (KJV)

I WAS OUTSIDE ON A run one day and for the first quarter mile or so, the wind was blowing so strongly against me, probably twenty-five miles an hour, I felt like I was running uphill. It was taking all of my energy.

Finally, I was able to turn. The path I run on is a big square. I knew that coming back, the last mile or so that wind would be blowing in my face again. I was dreading it.

But when I made the turn into the final home stretch, I was pleasantly surprised. The winds had changed direction. They were no longer blowing against me; they were blowing with me. It was a night-and-day difference. I could feel the winds propelling me forward.

I believe that's what will happen to you. The winds holding you back, causing you to struggle, are about to change in your direction.

You will enjoy times where you can feel God breathing in your direction. You will accomplish things that cause you to look back and say, "That had to be the hand of God. I'm not that smart. I'm not that talented."

What happened? The wind of Almighty God is blowing behind you. You may be in some kind of storm today with all kinds of things coming against you, but understand God is in control of those winds. Just a simple shift can make a huge difference. The same winds that are trying to defeat you, God can change their direction and cause them to be the very winds that will propel you into a higher level.

When my father went to be with the Lord, the winds tried to sink me, but God turned around and used the winds to push me into my divine destiny. What the enemy intends for your harm, God will turn around and use to your advantage.

I can sense in my spirit the winds are shifting. I can sense an increase in God's blessings. When you hear these winds blowing, you can't just sit back and think, *Ah, Joel. It will not happen to me. I never get good breaks.*

No, you will miss your moment of favor. When you hear the winds blowing, do like that little locust and say, "This is my time. I can hear the winds of God's favor. I will become everything God's created me to be."

You may have a lot coming against you, but have you ever realized that all it takes for the last to be first is the wind's changing direction? If it's all blowing this way, you may feel like you're last, way back here. But when the winds turn around and blow this way, all of a sudden you're first. What happens? The winds shift.

If you are in difficult times, instead of complaining and getting discouraged, you need to get up every morning and say it by faith: "Father, thank You that the winds are shifting in my direction. Thank You that the tide of this battle is turning."

Don't talk about the storm. Talk *to* your storm. Look at that situation and declare by faith, "You will not defeat me. I have moments of favor coming my way. I'm not only coming out. I'm coming out better off than I was before."

I love what David did when he faced Goliath. He could hear the treetops rustling. He'd been faithful in the wilderness for years. Now he could sense the winds were shifting—even though Goliath was two or three times his size.

Doubters tried to talk him out of it. "David, you don't have a chance. David, you will be hurt." Others couldn't hear the winds. They couldn't sense what he was sensing. When you know it's your time, don't get talked out of it. I've seen people sit back twenty years allowing other people to discourage them, talk them out of their dreams.

"Do you really think you can do that? I don't know if you have what it takes."

No, others don't know what's in you. They don't know what you're capable of because God didn't put the dream in them; He put it in you. When you hear the wind blowing, like that little locust, you should say, "This is my time."

If you'll get in the flow of God, you'll be amazed at how far you can go. When God's breathing in your direction, there's a supernatural ease. There's a grace to do things that you couldn't do before.

The doubters said, "David, you better not take a chance. Goliath, he's too big to hit."

David said, "I don't think so. He's too big to miss."

David spoke to his mountain. He said, "Goliath, this day I will defeat you and feed your head to the birds of the air."

What caused that little stone to slay the giant?

God breathed His life into it. The wind of Almighty God rose behind it. That's what happens when you make a leap of faith. You will accomplish things that you never thought possible.

You might say, "Joel, I don't see how this opportunity could happen for me. I don't have the money. I don't have the education. I don't have the talent."

The Scripture says it will not happen by our might or by our power. It will happen because of the breath of Almighty God. You know what's happening today? God's breathing in your direction.

Sometimes we think of a breath as just a little puff of air. That's not the way God breathes.

The Scripture says that when the Holy Spirit came, it was like a rushing, mighty wind. That's what I envision behind you: the force of Almighty God. Everywhere you go, you need to imagine the most powerful force in the universe breathing in your direction.

What happens when God breathes your way? Every enemy will be defeated, obstacles will be overcome, favor will increase, dreams will come to pass.

What happened? God breathed in your direction. A rushing, mighty wind is backing you up. Rise up in your authority and say, "You know what? I can hear the wind a-blowing so I'm stepping into the flow."

Things are shifting in your favor, my friend. Your future is filled with moments of favor, increase, promotion. God has already ordained before the foundation of the world the right people.

Time and chance are coming together for you. Get a vision for it. Raise your hopes. Don't miss your moment of favor. Even when it's difficult for you, just remember the same winds trying to defeat you are the winds God will use to push you to a new level.

If you'll go out each day with expectancy, knowing that God is breathing in your direction, I know you will rise higher and higher and see more of God's blessings and favor. And you'll live the life of victory He has in store.

❧ Today's Prayer to *It's Your Time* ❧

Father, thank You that the winds are shifting in my direction. Thank You that the tide of this battle is turning.

❧ Today's Thought to *It's Your Time* ❧

Imagine the most powerful force in the universe breathing in my direction, everywhere I go.

STAY GROUNDED IN FAITH

DAILY READING 1:11

SCRIPTURE READING TO *IT'S YOUR TIME*   PSALM 102

You will arise and have compassion on Zion
for it is time to show favor to her;
the appointed time has come.

PSALM 102:13 (NIV)

TYLER GREW UP POOR IN New Orleans in a household he's described as "scarred by abuse," so he ran away to Atlanta, where he lived homeless on the streets. It was a hard life. He has called his first twenty-eight years "unhappy and miserable."

I'm glad to say, Tyler found his new season of increase. Still, it is easy to get stuck in a rut like Tyler did. You don't expect anything. You don't grow. You don't press forward. And that's when negative thoughts come telling us that we've reached our limits and that we will never accomplish our goals. It's all downhill from here.

Don't ever believe those lies. God is a God of increase, not decrease. He never wants us to go backward; only forward. It is true that Job said, "The Lord gives and the Lord takes away."

Still, when it was all said and done, Job held on to his faith and ended up with twice what he had before. God restored back to him double. And sure, there are seasons where we're not seeing a lot of growth, seasons where we have to dig our heels in and fight the good fight of faith. But I can sense in my spirit that we are entering into new seasons of increase, new seasons of favor.

You have to believe, as Tyler does now, that no matter what's come against you, no matter how unfair it was, things are shifting in your favor. Tyler said the one thing that always kept him grounded was his faith. Every setback is simply a setup for a comeback. God not only wants to bring you out, He also wants to bring you out better off than you were before.

For Tyler, the season began turning when he started keeping a journal. He wrote about his feelings and his frustrations. He wrote about his experiences. But he was afraid that someone might read his journal. So Tyler made up characters in his journal. That way, no one would know the stories were about him.

Tyler's characters and stories launched his career as a writer and producer of plays, movies, and books. He now lives in a beautiful home on twelve acres outside Atlanta. His new home reflects the new season in his life. And so does his attitude about his success.

"I am a believer, and I know had I not been a person of faith, I couldn't be here in this place and I wouldn't be walking the path that I'm on now," he told an interviewer.

Tyler Perry believes that as low as a person can go, it is possible for the same person to go just as high. And even higher still. You may come from a history of abuse. Your relationships might have gone bad. Money might be scarce. Even so, you, too, have new seasons of increase coming.

God said He would make your enemies your footstools. I interpret this to mean that God will use the obstacles in your path, the stumbling blocks that would hold you back, as stepping-stones instead. He will use them to take you to a higher level.

It's as though somebody stuck out their foot to trip you, but God caused you to step right on top of it. Instead of going down, you went up!

You may be facing a sickness today. It was meant to harm you. It was meant to bring you down. But let me speak faith into you. That sickness will not defeat you. You have been armed with strength for every battle. The forces for you are greater than the forces against you.

I want to declare over you a new season in your health. The winds are shifting. Hard times may have held you down for a while but they will not last forever. When all is said and done, you will not be decreased; you will be increased.

You will step on top of these obstacles and use them as stepping-stones. You will come out stronger, more determined, with a greater faith than you've ever had before.

Get a vision for it. Let these seeds take root. New seasons in your health. New seasons in your pocketbook. New seasons in your relationships.

You still might have doubts: "Ah, Joel. My business is so slow. The economy is really hurting me."

No, God is not limited by the economy. God is not limited by our education or our lack of it. God is not limited by the environment we were raised in.

God is limited by our beliefs. I'm asking you to believe that things are shifting in your favor.

✖ Today's Prayer to *It's Your Time* ✖

Father, I believe things are shifting in my favor. I believe my season has come.

✖ Today's Thought to *It's Your Time* ✖

God has seasons in which supernatural doors will open, seasons in which I will accomplish things I never thought possible, seasons in which I will see great things begin to happen.

DECLARE THAT IT'S YOUR SEASON

DAILY READING 1:12

SCRIPTURE READING TO *IT'S YOUR TIME*   1 KINGS 18:41–42

Then Elijah said to Ahab, "Go up, eat and drink, for there is the sound of abundance of rain."

1 KINGS 18:41 (NKJ)

THERE HAD BEEN A DROUGHT for three and a half years. People were in desperate need of water. Elijah went to King Ahab and said, "I hear the sound of the abundance of rain."

In fact, there wasn't a cloud in the sky when he said that. There wasn't rain in the distance. It wasn't thundering. But Elijah could sense what was coming long before it arrived.

I can imagine Ahab looking at him and thinking, *What's wrong with him? There's no rain. It's not thundering. The heat must be getting to him.*

Elijah didn't hear it physically, in the natural. He heard it down in his spirit. And he was bold enough to announce it.

When you sense it's your season, you need to declare it. Words have creative power. You need to hear it and so does the enemy. You may not feel well, but it's good to announce, "Health is coming my way. I will live and not die."

People may look at you like Ahab looked at Elijah and think, *What's wrong with them? They don't look well. They look sick.*

But they can't hear the sound. They can't sense what you're sensing. They're just looking in the natural. And don't be surprised if your mind tells you things like, "You're just kidding yourself. You will never get well."

Just answer back, "Yes I will. I can hear it down in here."

Negative voices may say, "You'll never be debt-free."

But you can respond, "I can hear the sound of abundance."

Doubts may tell you, "You will never be married."

But you can hear the sound of God's favor, "Sure I will. I may not be able to see it, but I can sense victory, promotion, divine connections, supernatural opportunities—they're coming my way."

You still may not see how a new season of increase could happen for you.

That's because you are sensing the wrong things. You are sensing defeat, failure, mediocrity. That will only draw in negative feelings. It's like you're inviting negative forces into your life. You need to listen to these new sounds.

I can see over you an abundance of favor, an abundance of good breaks, an abundance of health, abundance in your finances, and an abundance of victory.

God is a God of abundance. He's saying today, "This is your season. This is your set time for favor." Why don't you let that seed of hope take root in your heart?

When those negative thoughts come telling you that it never will change, you never will be healthy, you never will get out of that mess; just do like Elijah and learn to announce your faith in a new season of increase.

✎ Today's Prayer to *It's Your Time* ✎

Father, I know my hour of deliverance is on its way. I may have a lot of turmoil, but I know everything will be all right.

✑ Today's Thought to *It's Your Time* ✑

I may not be able to see it, but I can sense victory, promotion, divine connections, supernatural opportunities—they're coming my way.

LET GOD'S SEED OF HOPE TAKE ROOT

---✧---

DAILY READING 1:13

SCRIPTURE READING TO *IT'S YOUR TIME*   LUKE 1:26–38

> *"Don't be afraid, Mary,"* the angel told her, *"for you have found favor with God!"*
>
> LUKE 1:30 (NLT)

MY FATHER'S SISTER MARY STRUGGLED with epilepsy. She'd have convulsions and terrible headaches. It was crippling her life. At one point an infection caused her to hallucinate. Her mind was not clear. She had been in the hospital for a long time. Then, she went home and fell into a coma. She couldn't recognize people. She couldn't feed herself. She needed twenty-four-hour care.

My father was living in another city and traveling so much that he did not realize how sick Mary had become. One day his mother, my grandmother, called to tell him of Mary's condition. Daddy was scheduled to go out of town for a week or so. But that next morning while he was praying, God spoke to him. Not out loud, but deep inside.

My father recalled this very distinct phrase: *The hour of Mary's deliverance has come.*

Notice, there's a set time for favor, a set time for increase, even a set time for deliverance. After my father finished praying, he opened his Bible and flipped through it. He randomly pointed to a scripture, hoping that God would give him a sign.

We've all done this before. It certainly doesn't always work. But this day he pointed to Luke 1:30, which says, "Don't be afraid, Mary, for you have found favor with God!"

He knew God was saying, *This is Mary's season.*

That morning, my father drove two hundred and forty miles from Houston to Dallas. When he went in Mary's room, it was dark, the lights were off, and the shades were pulled. Mary didn't even recognize him. Her hair was matted. Her eyes were glossy.

A holy anger came over my father. He went to the window shades, opened them, and said, "God is light. Let light in this room." He looked at Mary and said sternly, "Don't tell me God did this to my sister." He began to pray and pray and then he whispered, "Mary, I want you to get up out of this bed."

She immediately sat up. She hadn't walked in months. But that moment she rose from bed and walked around the house. Her mind cleared. She spoke to my father.

That same day she sat at the dinner table and fed herself. That same day she no longer needed her medicine. She sent away her twenty-four-hour care.

What happened? God shifted things in Mary's favor. Her set time for deliverance had come. My father asked, "Mary, why did you get up out of bed so quickly?"

She said, "Because I heard God tell me to get up."

My father corrected her: "No, Mary. I told you to get up."

She was adamant: "No, I heard God tell me to get up."

"No, Mary," my father insisted. "I was standing over you. I said 'Mary, get up.' "

Mary would not back down.

"Listen here, John," she said. "I heard the Creator of the universe. I heard Almighty God. He told me to get up out of that bed. And when I heard His voice, every fiber of my being came alive. It was God's voice!"

When you stay in faith, God will cause you to hear what you need to hear. Later, Mary wrote in her book that even though her mind was unclear for months, even though she was going in and out of consciousness, deep down inside she could sense something good was coming.

She could sense that one day she would be totally free; one day she would live a normal, healthy life.

If you listen way down on the inside, even in your dark hours, you will hear God whispering, "Something better is on the horizon."

Even when it looks impossible, you'll hear that still, small voice telling you, "I can turn it around. I can do what men can't do."

When everybody else is saying you're done, it's over, it never will be better; down in your spirit God will be saying, "I have a new beginning. I can resurrect those dead dreams. Your best days are still out in front of you."

Mary sensed what was coming long before it arrived. She heard the abundance of rain even when there wasn't a cloud in the sky. She was walking by faith and not by sight.

And I believe it's these little rays of hope, it's these little thoughts of faith that allow God to work in our lives. You don't have to have great faith. You don't have to understand all the theology and have all the answers if you will just let a little seed of God's hope take root in your heart.

✻ Today's Prayer to *It's Your Time* ✻

Father, thank You for turning my life around and putting hope in my heart.

✻ Today's Thought to *It's Your Time* ✻

This is my season.

GOD HAS YOUR SET TIMES

DAILY READING 1:14

SCRIPTURE READING TO *IT'S YOUR TIME*   MATTHEW 17:14–20

"You don't have enough faith," Jesus told them. "I tell you the truth, if you had faith even as small as a mustard seed, you could say to this mountain, 'Move from here to there,' and it would move. Nothing would be impossible."

MATTHEW 17:20 (NLT)

I RECEIVED A LETTER a while back from a lady whose neck was broken in a car accident. She had several surgeries that she hoped would improve her condition, but it grew worse. She was in constant pain. Her husband stayed home months and months to take care of her. She felt bad he'd been home that long. She finally talked him into going back to work. He reluctantly agreed.

One day while she was home alone, she was feeling depressed. She was in so much pain, she decided to end her life. She couldn't walk on her own, but she thought she could scoot out of her chair. She planned on crawling to the gun cabinet where her husband, a big hunter, kept his firearms.

But when she rose from the chair, she lost her balance and fell. She knocked over an end table and landed flat on her back, unable to move. She'd knocked the remote control for the television onto the floor and the batteries came out. As that happened, the remote changed channels on the television.

Wouldn't you know it? The channel just happened to be one on which I was ministering.

Later, this lady would recall that she had lost her faith after many years of believing her health would return. At one point she had that seed of hope. But it had been so long and she had been through so many setbacks, she felt like she had lost her faith.

Jesus said, "If you have faith even as small as a mustard seed." That's one of the smallest seeds, but that's all God needs to work with.

We may write Him off, but He never writes us off. Even when this woman didn't think God was working, her set time for deliverance was on its way. Her set time for favor was coming. She was flat on her back, unable to move. Her first thought was, *Oh, great. I'm dying here and now I have to listen to this TV preacher to add to my misery.*

But God works in mysterious ways. That day I was talking about how God can turn around any situation, and how He can turn your darkest hour into your brightest hour. And how nothing is too hard when we believe.

Hearing my words, this lady began to feel a peace that she'd never felt before.

"I couldn't move my body, couldn't open my eyes, but I could feel tears of joy running down my cheeks," she recalled.

Eventually, her husband came home and found her in a deep, deep sleep. After he woke her and checked her out, he made the comment, "It looks like you had an accident with the remote control."

She smiled and said, "It was no accident."

That day was a turning point. That day she began to get better. A new hope filled her heart.

My friend, God has your set times for deliverance. He has your set times for favor, your set times for increase. You may not have seen it in the past, but don't get discouraged. It's on its way. God's already lined up the right people, the right opportunities, the right breaks that you need. He has it all planned out.

✎ Today's Prayer to *It's Your Time* ✎

Father, I can hear the sound of abundance. I announce my faith in a new season of increase.

✎ Today's Thought to *It's Your Time* ✎

As long as I stay in faith, everything will be all right.

REMIND GOD OF WHAT YOU'VE DONE

DAILY READING 1:15

SCRIPTURE READING TO *IT'S YOUR TIME*   2 KINGS 20:1–11

> *"Go back to Hezekiah, the leader of my people. Tell him,*
> *"This is what the LORD, the God of your father David,*
> *says: "I have heard your prayer and seen your tears. I*
> *will heal you, and three days from now you will get out*
> *of bed and go to the Temple of the LORD.*
>
>   2 KINGS 20:5 (NLT)

THE OLD TESTAMENT OFFERS THE story of Hezekiah. He had been very sick. He had something similar to what doctors now call shingles. They didn't have the medicines or antibiotics that we have today. His health was going downhill in a hurry.

Hezekiah asked Isaiah the Prophet to come in and tell him what was about to happen. Isaiah said, "Hezekiah, here's the word of the LORD to you; 'Set your house in order. You will not live. You will die.' "

That's not exactly the word Hezekiah was hoping for. But I love the fact that he didn't give up and accept defeat. He could have thought, *God is God and He said I will die. I guess it's over for me.* But no, the Scripture says, "He turned his face toward the wall," and he began to remind God of everything good he had done.

He said, "Remember . . . how I have walked before you faithfully and with wholehearted devotion and have done what is good in your eyes."

Hezekiah pleaded his case. When you're in difficult times it's good to remind God what you've done.

"God, I kept my family in church. God, I've gone the extra mile to help others. I've given. I've served. I've been faithful."

In your own time of need you should call in all those seeds you've sown. If you have other family members, parents, grandparents, who loved God, just remind Him.

"God, my mother was a praying woman. You know that lady honored You. God, You know my grandparents. They had a heart after You."

What you're saying is, "God, we have a history with You." That's why in the Old Testament they prayed to the God of Abraham, the God of Isaac, and the God of Jacob. They were reminding God, "Here's how we've honored You."

Every time you come to church, every time you watch a service, you are storing up mercy for you and your family. You can look back and remind God, "I went to church. I was busy but, God, I brought my family to church, spent the gas money, took time to honor You."

It makes a difference when you put God first in your life. This is what Hezekiah was doing. He turned his face toward the wall and he asked God for His mercy. Before Isaiah left the temple, before he even left the building, God spoke to him again and said, "I want you to go back to Hezekiah and tell him I've changed my mind. I will not give him another year. I will not give him five years. I will not give him ten years. You tell him I will add fifteen years to his life."

My friend, God is into increase, not decrease. With our faith we can change God's mind. Think about it: One moment Hezekiah has a death sentence, not from a doctor, but from Almighty God. Then five minutes later things have shifted. God made an adjustment. Now all of sudden Hezekiah has fifteen more years of life.

What happened? Hezekiah entered into a new season, a season of increase. When did it happen? When did his set time for favor come? When he believed, when he expected God's goodness.

The Scripture says when he heard the good news, Hezekiah took off his grave clothes and he put on his praise clothes. He began to thank God that health was on its way. He thanked God for delivering him into a new season.

And I'm sure people looked at him and said, "Hezekiah, you sure look happy but you don't look any different to us. You still look sick. You still look weak and pale."

He likely said, "I may not look any different, I may not feel any different, but I can sense it down in here. I have a promise from Almighty God and I know the winds have shifted in my favor."

I can imagine Hezekiah walking through the temple singing that old song, "I've got a feeling everything is gonna be alright."

People would wonder, *Why is he singing? Doesn't he know he's about to die?*

No, he has a different report. He knows God made an adjustment. The winds changed directions. His set time for favor had come.

Isn't it interesting that God could have added just a year? That would have been nice. God could have added five years. That would have been great. But as a God of abundance, He said, "Hezekiah, I will give you fifteen more years. I will do more than you can even ask or think."

You may have hit hard times. You may have been through the fire and flood. But God says, "Favor is coming your way."

He's making adjustments. Things are shifting. You may not see how it could happen in the natural. You may not be able to explain it. But deep down inside, the seed has taken root.

Let me declare it over you: new seasons of increase, new seasons in your health, new seasons in your finances, new seasons in your relationships.

God is saying, "This is your set time for favor." You may have been rejected in the past, but you will be accepted in the future. You may have been pushed down in days gone by, but you will be lifted up. God will make your enemies your footstools.

You may have struggled for years, but you are about to enter into that anointing of ease. Why? This is your season. The winds have changed direction.

Do as Hezekiah did and shed your grave clothes. Get rid of that negative, defeated, not-going-to-happen mentality and put on an attitude of faith, expectancy, praise, thanksgiving. All through the day thank God that new seasons are on their way. Thank Him that your set time for favor is here. Thank Him that your hour of deliverance has come.

If you do this, you will see the wind of God's blessings and favor flow into your life in ways you have never seen before.

✖ Today's Prayer to *It's Your Time* ✖

Father, thank You for my time of favor and my hour of deliverance.

✖ Today's Thought to *It's Your Time* ✖

I will put God first in my life.

THE LORD IS YOUR FATHER AND PROVIDER

DAILY READING 1:16

SCRIPTURE READING TO *IT'S YOUR TIME*   1 JOHN 3:1–10

How great is the love the Father has lavished on us, that we should be called children of God! And that is what we are! . . .

1 JOHN 3:1 (NIV)

THE FORMER BASEBALL STAR JESSE Barfield and his wife, Marla, have been with our church for many years. Jesse led the major leagues with forty home runs while playing for the Toronto Blue Jays. He later played for the New York Yankees, where he also was known for having the strongest throwing arm in baseball.

Jesse is the most naturally talented, gifted athlete I've ever seen. Sometimes during the off-season we played basketball together. And even though that's not his main sport, he was ten times better than the rest of us. He's in his own league.

He and Marla have several children. I've watched them grow up. Their oldest son, Josh, was a star baseball player in high school. He went to college and did great. He was drafted into the minor leagues and excelled there. A few years ago he was called up to the big leagues and now he's excelling at the highest level, playing professional baseball. Jesse's younger son, Jeremy, also made the big leagues.

Statistics tell us that only one child in a million will ever make it to the big leagues. But what's interesting is Josh's and Jeremy's success in the big leagues doesn't surprise me. I know their father. I've seen Jesse play. I've witnessed firsthand his strength, his speed, his ability to hit.

You've heard the saying, "Like father, like son." Baseball is in their DNA. Jesse's athletic skills were passed down.

I know who your Father is, too. That is why I believe there is no limit to what you can do. There is no obstacle you can't overcome. I've seen your Father's accomplishments. There's no challenge that's too much for you. Your Father always succeeds.

❧ Today's Prayer to *It's Your Time* ❧

Father, You are the Lord my Provider, with Your support I will succeed.

❧ Today's Thought to *It's Your Time* ❧

I know who my Father is. That is why I believe there is no limit to what I can do.

YOUR POTENTIAL IS WAITING
TO BE RELEASED

DAILY READING 1:17

SCRIPTURE READING TO *IT'S YOUR TIME*   LUKE 6:37–42

Give, and it will be given to you. A good measure, pressed down, shaken together and running over, will be poured into your lap. . . .

LUKE 6:38 (NIV)

WHEN MICHAEL JORDAN FIRST TRIED out for his school's varsity basketball team, he didn't make it. Michael was a freshman. He was still only five feet, ten inches tall. There was only one open spot on varsity. Another freshman who was eight inches taller won it.

At that point Michael Jordan wasn't super-coordinated and super-athletic. But there was a gene locked up in his DNA that was about to be released, a gene that would make him eight inches taller and give him an incredible ability to jump and soar through the air.

Michael Jordan could have gotten discouraged as a freshman. He could have thought, *Basketball is just not for me.* But something deep down on the inside kept telling him, "This is for you. You have what it takes. This is what you were born to do." His destiny was calling out to him. It was in his DNA.

Even though he went through that rejection and additional setbacks, he realized that other people didn't determine his destiny.

Other people didn't know what God put in him. He kept believing. He kept being his best, kept pressing forward, and one day that gene activated. He became one of the greatest basketball players of our time.

All of us have gifts just waiting to be activated. For thirty-five years I didn't know there was a minister in me. I didn't know I could do it. I'm naturally more quiet and reserved. I liked being behind the scenes. But when my father went to be with the Lord in 1999, one of those genes that God put in me before the foundation of time, all of a sudden it activated. All of a sudden it came alive, and deep down on the inside I knew that ministering was what I was supposed to do. Looking back, I realize this wasn't a surprise to God. He had preprogrammed the abilities in me before I ever arrived here. All of our days have been written in His book.

I'd tell Victoria, "I'm not a minister. I can't speak in public." She'd tell me time and again, "Yes, Joel. You can. One day you will pastor the church."

Still, I'd deny it: "No, Victoria. It's just not in me."

Now I know it was in my God-given DNA. That gene was lying dormant because it was not the right time. When the right season came along, all of a sudden I had a desire to step up and be a minister. I had to make a decision: Was I willing to step out of my comfort zone? Could I believe in myself as pastor? Was I fit for the calling? Or should I just sit back, play it safe, and stay right where I was, letting the opportunity pass me by?

I took that step of faith, and I really believe that's when the gene activated and I stepped in to my divine destiny. Now I know I'm doing what I was born to do. I know this is one of the reasons God put me here.

Some of the genes that God preprogrammed in you are about to be activated. Like me, you will accomplish things that you never thought possible. You will see new talents, new levels of ability, new levels of wisdom and insight, new levels in your career, new levels of success.

✥ Today's Prayer to *It's Your Time* ✥

Father in heaven, I receive Your Word into my heart today. Thank You for choosing to bless me so that I can be a blessing to others.

✥ Today's Thought to *It's Your Time* ✥

I will take a step of faith today.

YOU HAVE GOD'S DNA

DAILY READING 1:18

SCRIPTURE READING TO *IT'S YOUR TIME*   2 CORINTHIANS 5:11–20

> *Therefore, if anyone is in Christ, he is a new creation; old things have passed away; behold, all things have become new.*
>
> 2 CORINTHIANS 5:17 (NKJ)

BORN POOR IN THE SEGREGATED South, Robert J. "Bob" Brown had few advantages in life. But he had two things going for him: He was raised in the church by his grandparents, and he had his Almighty Father's DNA.

After a brief career in law enforcement, Bob opened his own public relations firm in a small North Carolina town. That led to him working with big corporations across the country. In the 1960s, he served as a bridge between his clients and the leaders of the civil rights movement.

Later, this great-grandson of slaves served four years in the White House as a special assistant to the president of the United States. Today, he has a charity that sends millions of books to poor children in South Africa each year.

Bob Brown never knew his father. His mother left him with her parents to raise him. Yet he was preprogrammed for victory. He was equipped with everything he needs.

Why don't you get that down on the inside, too? Tell yourself, "I have been preprogrammed for victory. I don't have to worry about my future. I have the right genes—the DNA of Almighty God."

∼ Today's Prayer to *It's Your Time* ∼

Father in heaven, I trust that You have great things in store for my future. I surrender every area of my mind, will, and emotions as I wait on You.

∼ Today's Thought to *It's Your Time* ∼

I will prepare my heart and mind to receive the increase and blessing God has in store for me.

YOU ARE A PERSON OF DESTINY

DAILY READING 1:19

SCRIPTURE READING TO *It's Your Time*　　　　　HAGGAI 2:1–9

> *"The glory of this present house will be greater than the glory of the former house," says the LORD Almighty. "And in this place I will grant peace," . . .*
>
> HAGGAI 2:9 (NIV)

As CHILDREN WE TRAVELED AROUND the country with my father on his speaking engagements. Very often we'd get preferential treatment because of his good name. People loved my dad. I could hear them whispering about us, "They are John Osteen's children."

We were in Chicago at this big hotel where my father was speaking to a group in the ballroom. I was about ten or eleven years old. I really loved the milk shakes at the hotel's coffee shop. I was walking through the lobby with my little sister, April, and we stopped in front of the coffee shop to look at a picture of those milk shakes. They had an advertisement on the wall of all their bakery items.

As we were standing there, a lady came up and said, "Aren't you John Osteen's children?"

I said, "Yes, ma'am. We are."

She said, "Well, if it'd be okay with you, I want to buy you each one of those milk shakes." I thought about her offer for two-tenths of a second.

"That would be fine," I said.

She bought us milk shakes, and I knew it was because of our father. I was so proud. After that, I walked through the lobby knowing I was something special. I was his son.

For the next three days I hung out in front of that coffee shop. Anytime I saw anyone who halfway looked like they were attending the conference, I would stand up there and stare at that milk shake, hoping they would buy me one.

Another lady did stop one day. She said, "Aren't you John Osteen's child?"

I smiled real big, thinking, *Here it comes.*

"Yes, ma'am. I am!"

"Well, good," she said. "Maybe you can tell me where the ballroom is."

I was so disappointed. I pointed at the restrooms and ran off the other way.

Studies tell us that a male child usually gets his identity from his father. Maybe you weren't raised with a good father figure. Maybe you were passed from home to home and had a lot of negativity and people trying to beat you down. But that doesn't have to stop you.

Understand that you have a Heavenly Father. Don't go around feeling inferior because of what someone did or didn't give you. Don't feel intimidated. You have the right genes.

You are not an accident. You are a person of destiny. There are gifts and talents in you just waiting to be released. You have potential that you've not yet tapped into. You must shake off any feelings of inferiority or low self-esteem. Put your shoulders back. Hold your head up high. You are a child of the Most High God. You have His royal blood flowing through your veins.

❧ Today's Prayer to *It's Your Time* ❧

Father in heaven, thank You for making me Your child of destiny.

❧ Today's Thought to *It's Your Time* ❧

If I stay in faith, God will amaze me with his goodness!

GET IN AGREEMENT WITH GOD

DAILY READING 1:20

SCRIPTURE READING TO *It's Your Time*   JEREMIAH 1:1–10

*"I knew you before I formed you in your mother's womb.
Before you were born I set you apart
and appointed you as my prophet to the nations."*
                                        JEREMIAH 1:5 (NLT)

I AM WHO I AM today in part because Victoria spoke faith into me when I wasn't sure of following my father as pastor. When we hear words of faith and victory, something resonates on the inside. Something down in here says, "This is for me. This is who I am. This is what I was created to be." Our Spirit Person comes alive.

It's so important for you to get around people who will stir up those seeds of greatness. Don't surround yourself with naysayers. Life is too short to hang around negative, critical, cynical, skeptical, judgmental, small-minded, jealous people. . . . Did I leave out anything?

Find some dreamers, people who will build you up, people who will celebrate your victories, not people who will criticize and be jealous any time you succeed. I believe today can be a new beginning. I believe your dreams are being restored. Fresh vision is being released. New hope is being activated.

Your best days are not behind you, they are still out in front of you. You may have been through disappointments. You may feel that others have weighed you down, or that your own poor choices have cursed your future, but remember this: Before anyone could put a curse on you, God put a blessing on you, and the blessing always overrides the curse.

I declare that every good thing God has put in you will come to fulfillment. Every gift, every talent, every dream, every desire will come to pass. I declare you will fulfill your purpose. You will fulfill your God-given destiny and become all He has created you to be. I declare you will overcome every obstacle. The strongholds of the past are being broken off of you. The negative things in your family line for generations will no longer affect you.

I declare the seeds of increase, the seeds of success, the seeds of promotion are taking a new root. The DNA of Almighty God will spring forth in your life in a greater way. You will see new seasons of increase, new seasons of God's blessings, new season of His favor.

✄ Today's Prayer to *It's Your Time* ✄

Father, thank You for the dreams and desires You've given me so that I can discover the destiny You have in mind for me.

✄ Today's Thought to *It's Your Time* ✄

My destiny lies within those things I most love to do.

PART TWO

IT'S TIME FOR FAVOR

PRAY BOLD PRAYERS

DAILY READING 2:1

SCRIPTURE READING TO *IT'S YOUR TIME*   PROVERBS 28:1–10

The wicked man flees though no one pursues,
but the righteous are as bold as a lion.
       PROVERBS 28:1 (NIV)

ONE OF MY MOST CREATIVE friends nearly didn't have the chance to share his talents with the world. His mother became pregnant with him when she was seventeen and unmarried. She was white. His father was black. This was 1971 in a small Iowa town.

The girl's parents strongly encouraged her to have an abortion. In fact, they gave her an ultimatum: Either abort the baby or get out of their home. She chose to have the baby.

Once a promising concert pianist, she ended up in San Diego, eight months' pregnant, alone and confused, battling a drug addiction.

A lady talked to her on the street one day about God's love and forgiveness. And that day, she made a decision for Christ. The lady gave her a Bible. She flipped through it, saw the name Israel time and again. She thought to herself, *I will name my baby Israel.* She didn't know much about God. She didn't know how to pray. But she said boldly, "God, I'm committing my little baby to You. I'm asking You to use him to do great things."

The teen mother passed her musical gifts on to her child. God took care of the rest. Her son grew up with incredible musical gifts. He could play practically any instrument. He could write songs. He could arrange music. As he grew older, he began writing worship songs that declared God's goodness. He put together his own band and supernatural doors opened.

Today, we all know and love Israel Houghton. He is one of the great worship leaders and great songwriters of our time. Israel and his band, New Breed, have won Grammy Awards and praise around the world for their uplifting music.

That's what happens when you pray bold prayers. Israel could have become a statistic. He could have just foundered, never finding his purpose. But I believe that because this mother dared pray a bold prayer, his life was set on an extraordinary path.

God wants to bless you. He wants to enlarge your territory. Will you be bold enough to ask Him each day for more influence? Ask God to help you be a bigger blessing. That's not a selfish request. The Scripture says, "You have not because you ask not." If we are to see the full blossoming of His favor, we have to learn to pray bold prayers.

Today's Prayer to *It's Your Time*

Father, I ask for Your favor, Your blessings, and Your increase.

Today's Thought to *It's Your Time*

God expects me to ask for His favor.

ASK GOD TO FULFILL YOUR HIGHEST HOPES

DAILY READING 2:2

SCRIPTURE READING TO *IT'S YOUR TIME*   MATTHEW 7:7–11

*"Keep on asking, and you will receive what you ask for.
Keep on seeking, and you will find. Keep on knocking,
and the door will be opened to you."*
                                        MATTHEW 7:7 (NLT)

JAMIE WAS SEVEN YEARS OLD and living on her family's farm when she told her dad that she dreamed of having her own little calf. As it happened, one of their cows was about to give birth, but Jamie's father had already decided not to keep any more cows. He planned on selling this calf and any others that came along.

But for some reason little Jamie really wanted to keep this calf. She pleaded and pleaded with her dad day after day, "Please, Daddy, let me keep this cow. Please make an exception, just one more cow for me."

After a couple of weeks she wore down her father and he finally said, "Okay, Jamie, I'll make a deal with you. If the cow is black, you can keep it, but if it's spotted or brown like the rest of our cows, then we'll get rid of it."

Jamie agreed. Then, she started praying and asking God for that cow to be born black. Every night before she went to bed, she said, "God, thank you that this little calf will be as black as can be and there won't be any doubt that it's mine."

That's uncommon faith. Most of us adults would never pray anything like that. We would think that's far out. That's radical. That's extreme.

But I've found that radical faith gets radical results. Extreme faith gets extreme results. A few weeks later this little calf was born. It was black, and right between its eyes there was a white patch that formed a big *J*.

It was as if God put a big stamp on it, to mark that calf as Jamie's. When you release your faith in uncommon ways, you'll see God do uncommon things. Some people never ask God for their dreams. Maybe you've asked for everyone else's, but you need to ask for what God has put in your heart. And in your quiet time, when it's just between you and God, dare to ask Him for your deepest hopes, your greatest dreams.

✆ Today's Prayer to *It's Your Time* ✆

Father, thank You for helping me live my dreams and fulfill the destiny You created for me.

✆ Today's Thought to *It's Your Time* ✆

When I release my faith in uncommon ways, God will do uncommon things.

GOD HOLDS YOUR WORLD IN HIS HAND

DAILY READING 2:3

Scripture Reading to *It's Your Time*   Hebrews 11:8–17

It was by faith that Abraham obeyed when God called him to leave home and go to another land that God would give him as his inheritance. He went without knowing where he was going. And even when he reached the land God promised him, he lived there by faith—for he was like a foreigner, living in tents. And so did Isaac and Jacob, who inherited the same promise.

Hebrews 11:8–9 (NLT)

My friend Tom's daughter Shari was about three years old when something sharp fell on her hand and she lost the tips of two fingers. They rushed her to the emergency room and after they stopped the bleeding, a plastic surgeon examined Shari's fingers.

"I'm sorry," he told Tom. "There's nothing we can do to restore her fingers back to normal. She'll never have nails on those two fingers and they'll always be a little shorter."

The bones were severed. All they could do was a skin graft to try to make them look as smooth as possible, the surgeon said.

Tom was very respectful, but he told the doctor, "I believe that God can restore my little girl's fingers and make them normal again."

The surgeon, who'd grown up in another country without religion in his life, said, "That's fine if you want to believe it, but understand the bone is missing. They will never be the right length, and for sure she won't have fingernails."

Tom didn't argue, but he stuck with his beliefs.

When his wife, Ruth, came in, the doctor pulled her aside and said, "Your husband is in shock. He won't accept the fact that the tips of her fingers are permanently damaged."

The surgeon did the skin graft. Six weeks later they brought Shari back to check her fingers. When the doctor took off the bandages, his first words were, "Oh my God."

Alarmed, Tom said, "What's wrong?"

"The fingernails grew back," the surgeon said. "It looks like the fingers are the exact right length."

That was more than twenty years ago. To this day, Shari's fingers look perfectly normal. Her story always reminds me that we should never be afraid to ask God for uncommon blessings. I respect medical experts. But there is another expert who breathed life into us all. God made your body. He holds your world in His hand. He controls the universe.

Just as He can hold back the rain, He can heal a child. He can bring your dreams to pass. He can help you overcome your obstacles.

Dare to ask God for your greatest dreams and desires. Don't settle for a lesser dream. Deep down you may have a desire to become an author, to break an addiction, or to serve the needy in another country. But you may feel it could never happen. You may have been through disappointments. Maybe you've been praying for a long time and nothing has happened. Now, you've lost your enthusiasm so you're praying what I call "survival prayers."

God, just help me make it through the day.

Lord, help me deal with the boss tomorrow.

God, please make sure I don't get another speeding ticket.

There is nothing wrong with those prayers. But they are like asking the world's greatest surgeon to put a Band-Aid on your broken leg. The surgeon can do much, much more for you, if you would only have faith and ask for the very best treatment.

✌ Today's Prayer to *It's Your Time* ✌

Father, thank You for leading me beyond my wildest dreams and to my ultimate destiny.

✌ Today's Thought to *It's Your Time* ✌

I must ask so that I may receive.

DO YOU HAVE BLESSINGS WAITING TO BE RELEASED?

DAILY READING 2:4

SCRIPTURE READING TO *IT'S YOUR TIME*   JOSHUA 4

That day the LORD exalted Joshua in the sight of all Israel; and they revered him all the days of his life, . . .
JOSHUA 4:14 (NIV)

FRIEND, GOD WANTS TO DO the same thing for you that He did for Joshua. He wants to release His blessings and favor in such a way that it makes you a great parent, a great spouse, a great leader, a great employee, a great friend, a great businessperson. My Father would tell a story that Bruce Wilkinson used in a slightly different form in *The Prayer of Jabez*. Dad would encourage his church members to imagine a huge warehouse in Heaven run by Saint Peter, the keeper of the keys. As you walk down the halls, you see thousands and thousands of doors with names on them. Finally, you come to a door with your name on the plaque. That gets your attention. You halt and say to Saint Peter, "What is in there?"

He tries to downplay it. "Ah, nothing. You don't want to go in there."

"Sure I do," you insist. "My name is on the door."

After debating for a few minutes, you finally convince Saint Peter to let you go in. He opens the door. Inside you see row after row of boxes on shelves. You hurry over to open up one and then the realization comes: *These are blessings that belong to me but have never been released!*

The first is a box of favor that God wanted you to have last week. But you never asked.

The next is a big break that God prepared for you last month. But you forgot to ask for it.

Down the row, there is a box containing the book you wanted to write but gave up on. Beside it is the business you wanted to create. Then there is one containing the healing God planned for you.

Row after row of blessings, favors, good breaks, good ideas. They all belong to you, but God never released them because you never asked.

I don't know about you, but I want to make sure my warehouse is completely empty. I don't want to be greedy. I don't want to be selfish. I simply want all that belongs to me. I want to be everything God has created me to be. I want to have everything God intended for me to have.

Think of it this way: What if God had five blessings in store for you last week but you missed out because you were not praying boldly to Him?

A big break?

A good idea?

A profitable opportunity?

A person who'll change your life?

A chance to benefit others with your talents?

Those potential blessings are still stored in your heavenly warehouse. Only bold prayers will open the door to them. You may be so kindhearted and generous that you always pray for others, but you never ask God to fulfill your own dreams. It is good to help others. But every morning after you thank God for what He's done, after you thank Him for His goodness in your life, you should get in the habit of asking for His favor in a bold way.

❧ Today's Prayer to *It's Your Time* ❧

Father God, I worship You today. You alone are worthy of all glory and honor. Thank You for pouring out Your favor and blessing on me. I open my heart and mind to receive everything You have in store for me.

❧ Today's Thought to *It's Your Time* ❧

When my needs are met, I should stretch to bless others.

DARE TO DREAM

DAILY READING 2:5

SCRIPTURE READING TO *IT'S YOUR TIME*   GENESIS 37:8–10

*Then he had another dream, and he told it to his broth-
ers. "Listen," he said, "I had another dream, and this
time the sun and moon and eleven stars were bowing
down to me."*

GENESIS 37:9 (NIV)

I HAVE A FRIEND WHO grew up in the African nation once known
as Zaire but now called the Democratic Republic of the Congo.
My friend was the seventh of ten siblings. They shared their home
with several cousins and other relatives. His father was head of the
school system in the capital city, where one in four people lived in
poverty.

This friend, who once dreamed of becoming a doctor, grew up
aware that many people were dying in his country because of in-
adequate medical care. Often, children and adults died from health
problems that were easily treatable if only they'd been somewhere
with up-to-date medical care.

As a young boy his heart was stirred. He couldn't stand seeing the suffering and sadness of his people. God put a dream in
his heart. One day, somehow, someway, he would return to make

things better. But how could that be possible? He was just one small boy.

Still, there was something different about this intelligent, athletic young man. He had no fear of praying bold prayers. Even as a little boy, he said, "God help me to help my people. God give me a way to bring this dream to pass."

Our far-out God took an unusual approach in my friend's case. Since he was an intelligent child, you might expect that God would have gone with the boy's game plan and helped him become a doctor.

Instead, God took this growing boy and just kept growing him. Taller and taller and taller. And taller still!

He grew so much that his father encouraged him to give up soccer for basketball. He struggled at first because his coordination could not keep up with his height. Though he was seven feet, two inches tall, he went to Georgetown University on an academic rather than an athletic scholarship. That was unheard of—a supernatural break.

He planned to study medicine so he could go back and help his people. But during his second year, the basketball coach, John Thompson, asked him to try out for the team. He not only made the squad, but he also became a star player. Later, he was drafted in the first round by the Denver Nuggets of the NBA.

Dikembe Mutombo, who later joined the Houston Rockets and attends our church, became one of the greatest defensive players in NBA history. He did not become a doctor, but he never gave up on his bold dream.

The critical need for better medical care in his native country was brought home to him once again when his mother died of a stroke in 1997. Ten years later, Mutombo opened a research and teaching hospital in his African hometown. He donated $15 million and raised millions more to build it. Then he named it after his mother, who taught him to always dream big.

God has a way to bring your dreams to pass if you'll dare be bold enough to ask. If God did it for Deke Mutombo, He can do it for you!

✑ Today's Prayer to *It's Your Time* ✑

Father, thank You for showing me that nothing is impossible with you.

✑ Today's Thought to *It's Your Time* ✑

The dreams God has given me are treasures worth living for.

ARE YOU STRETCHING YOUR FAITH?

SCRIPTURE READING TO *IT'S YOUR TIME*   1 CHRONICLES 4:9–10

> *Jabez cried out to the God of Israel, "Oh, that you would bless me and enlarge my territory! Let your hand be with me, and keep me from harm so that I will be free from pain." And God granted his request.*
>
> 1 CHRONICLES 4:10 (NIV)

IN THE OLD TESTAMENT STORY of Jabez, we learn that his name meant "pain, suffering, trouble" and "heartache." Unfortunately, the name suited him all too well. You see, in those ancient times, a person's name was much more significant than it is today. People tended to take on the traits of their given names. For instance, *Jacob* means "deceiver." And if you study the Bible, you'll find that Jacob cheated and deceived people.

On the other hand, the name *Joshua* means "savior." I'm sure courage and hope filled his heart because Joshua knew he was called to deliver God's people.

Knowing that, consider how Jabez must have felt. Every time someone said, "Hey, Jabez," they were saying, "Hey, trouble. Hey, sorrow. Hey, pain."

They were prophesying more defeat and failure. We don't know why Jabez's parents named him this. Maybe it was because the father abandoned the mother. Maybe she was so hurt and so angry she named him that. Maybe she had a difficult pregnancy or childbirth with him so she named him "pain, heartache, trouble."

You can imagine what Jabez had to put up with in school. The other kids probably gave him a hard time.

"Hey, there's Jabez. Here comes *trouble.*"

"What's up with you, man? Why would your parents name you that?"

His name could have put limits on his life. It could have affected his self-image and made him feel insecure and inferior. But the Scripture says Jabez was more honorable than any others in his family. It doesn't tell us much about him except one little prayer he prayed. From this prayer, we can see there was something special about Jabez. In spite of his rough upbringing, in spite of his self-image constantly being attacked, Jabez looked up to the heavens and said, "God, I'm asking that You would bless me indeed."

Think of the nerve of that prayer. He said, "God, I've had a lot of things come against me. Life hasn't treated me fairly. I'm off to a rough start. But God, I know You're a good God. I know You have a great plan for my life. So I'm asking You to bless me indeed."

Notice the *indeed.* It's significant. He wasn't saying, "God, I'm asking You to bless me *a little bit.* Bless me *average.* Bless me *ordinary.*" No, Jabez said, "God, I'm asking for abundance. I'm asking for overflow. Bless me *indeed.*"

Jabez asked for abundance. He asked for overflow. *Bless me indeed!*

Do you see his boldness? What right did he have to pray that prayer? He was supposed to be destined for heartache, pain, trouble. He was supposed to live defeated and depressed. But old Jabez shook off that defeated mentality. He said in effect, "It doesn't matter what someone has named me. It doesn't matter what it looks like in the natural. I know who I am. I'm a child of the Most High God and my destiny is to be blessed."

Jabez went on to say not only "bless me," but also "God, enlarge my territory." He was saying, "God, go beyond the norm. Go beyond my borders. Give me extraordinary favor. God, let me see abundance in my life."

The last thing we hear from Jabez is found at the end of verse 10. Surely, God would say, "Jabez, would you quit bothering me? Do you know what your name means? You will not be blessed. Your own parents said you're headed for trouble and heartache."

Instead, the verse says simply, "And God granted him his request."

That is the kind of God we serve. If you pray bold prayers, God will do bold things in your life. You may have had a rough beginning. Maybe you weren't treated fairly either. You've had some setbacks. But if Jabez were here today, he would tell you, "Don't settle where you are. If you'll dare ask, God will bless you indeed."

If the psalmist David were around today, he would say, "God can lift you out of that low place. He can put a new song in your heart. He can put a spring back in your step. He can set you on high."

Maybe you've made mistakes, poor choices. You feel like you're washed up or that you are supposed to just endure life. But God is saying, "If you'll ask, I'll give you a new beginning."

Maybe you've been hurt in a relationship. Somebody did you wrong and it didn't work out. Now you think you'll never really be happy. Why don't you be bold like Jabez and say, "God, I know it looks like it's over. It looks like my best days are behind me. But I believe you are a far-out God. So I'm asking for You to bring somebody great into my life, the perfect person for me."

No matter what's come against you, if you'll be bold enough to ask, the rest of your life can be better than ever before. When you awaken each day and say the prayer of Jabez, "God, bless me indeed. Enlarge my territory," you are off on the right foot.

His prayer says, "God, I know You love me. I know good things are in store for me. So I'm asking today for Your favor, for Your increase, for Your blessings in my life."

That is not being selfish. That's showing God that you're depending on Him. Maybe you are asking God to bless you, but you have neglected to add the "indeed." You need a bigger vision.

"God, I'm asking You to bless me in unusual ways; not average, not ordinary. God, I'm asking for supernatural increase."

I pray every day for God's unprecedented favor. That's favor like we've never seen before. I've learned not to pray small prayers. They set limits.

You may be living in a little apartment today, but deep down something on the inside says, "I'm made for more than this. I'm supposed to own my own home."

Dare to ask.

Maybe you're struggling in your health and you could easily learn to live with it. But deep down inside something says, "I'm supposed to be well. I'm supposed to be free from this pain."

Dare to ask.

Or maybe you have a good job. But in your heart of hearts you know one day you're supposed to own your own business. Don't settle where you are. Every day just say, "Father, I'm asking for supernatural opportunities. God, give me ways to bring this dream to pass."

It may not happen overnight, but stay in faith.

Today's Prayer to *It's Your Time*

Father, I'm asking for supernatural opportunities!

Today's Thought to *It's Your Time*

I will not settle for where I am, I will stay in faith and keep striving to live my dreams.

CHOOSE THRIVING OVER STRIVING

$$\sim$$

SCRIPTURE READING TO *IT'S YOUR TIME*   JEREMIAH 29:10–23

> *For I know the plans I have for you, "declares the LORD," plans to prosper you and not to harm you, plans to give you hope and a future.*
>
> JEREMIAH 29:11 (NIV)

DO YOU KNOW WHAT GENERAL Electric, Hewlett Packard, IBM, and Microsoft have in common? All of these innovative American corporations originated during a severe economic downturn or a depression.

Challenging times have served as catalysts for creativity, innovation, and accomplishment throughout human history. Yet when times grow tough and things aren't going our way, it's tempting to just hunker down. Thoughts of increase and moving forward are put on hold.

News reports of a sinking economy or personal problems of our own can tempt us to think, *If I can just hold on, maybe I can make it through another day, another month, another year.* If we're not careful, we develop this survival mentality. We stop releasing our faith. We stop believing we can rise any higher. We just try to maintain the status quo, to keep our heads above water, to break even.

But we're not supposed to break even. We're supposed to break through to a new level, to more of God's favor, to increase, to promotion.

I've known people who have been through tough times—maybe a relationship didn't work out or they experienced some kind of disappointment—and even though things improved, they never stopped thinking of themselves as survivors. I saw a guy wearing a T-shirt that said, "I survived Hurricane Katrina." I wanted to congratulate him for surviving one of history's worst storms, but then I wanted to tell him that you can't stay in survival mode. You can't always be the victim: *I just have to hold on.* No, you are not a survivor. You are more than a conqueror.

I realize some seasons are more difficult. Not every season is harvest. Sometimes we go through trying times where it seems like things are drying up and getting a little more challenging. Part of the problem is that we've heard so many stories about victims and survivors. Yet there are conquerors in every situation. Even in Hurricane Katrina, there were heroes.

High school principal Elmer Mullins and sheriff's captain Windy Swetman Jr. were in charge of a storm shelter during Hurricane Katrina. Nearly three hundred people came to their high school near Biloxi, Mississippi. They called it "a shelter of last resort" because it was in a flood plain. People went there only if they had nowhere else to go.

Some of them swam in. Others couldn't make it. The principal and the sheriff had to go out in a school bus, in the middle of the storm, to rescue three deputies and their two police dogs caught in floodwaters.

They didn't just hunker down. They didn't just hang on. They didn't just survive. They went out and conquered that storm.

A scripture in Jeremiah says if we'll give the Lord our trust and confidence, God will prosper us even in the desert. He'll prosper us even in difficult times. That means when others are going under, God says you will go over.

✤ Today's Prayer to *It's Your Time* ✤

Father, thank You for helping me to thrive through my faith in You.

✤ Today's Thought to *It's Your Time* ✤

If I give the Lord my trust and confidence, He will prosper me even in the desert.

THE FAITHFULNESS OF GOD

DAILY READING 2:8

SCRIPTURE READING TO *IT'S YOUR TIME*　　　　ISAIAH 54:11–17

> *No weapon formed against you shall prosper,* . . .
> ISAIAH 54:17 (NKJ)

MY FATHER HAD A FRIEND who was a very successful orange grower in Florida. He owned hundreds and hundreds of acres of groves. One winter forecasters predicted a hard freeze would hit. Such cold was rare for his part of the state. He and other growers feared a freeze would destroy their orange trees and wipe out their businesses.

Still, this grower was a man of great faith. He believed God could do anything. Just before the freeze, he went into his grove and marched around his trees, praying out loud, "God, I'm asking You to protect my crops and keep them from freezing." His friends and fellow growers thought he was behaving strangely. But later they wondered if he knew something they didn't.

The big freeze lasted more than twenty-four hours. Other growers worried the whole time that their crops would be destroyed. Our friend just kept thanking God for protecting his crops.

When the freeze ended, the groves all around his were destroyed. Every tree was dead. But his groves were untouched. Big healthy oranges hung on his trees. It looked like God had put a big blanket over his property.

The other growers were amazed. Those who'd made fun of him for praying in his groves said, "Next time, pray for our crops, too!"

God is well able to take care of us. He can prosper us even in the desert if we'll just be bold enough to believe. Scripture says, "No weapon that is formed against you will prosper." Disappointments and setbacks will come. But you don't have to get down and go into survival mode. Stay in faith and believe that God will protect you supernaturally. Believe that you will see His unprecedented favor.

Maybe business is slow. Others in your market are struggling. Why not thank God for bringing you new clients, giving you new opportunities, opening up supernatural doors?

Instead of getting discouraged and thinking, *Oh, man, the bad economy will hit me hard. My business will probably go down,* try thanking our Father for bringing you the best year ever! You might as well get ready for promotion, for divine connections, for supernatural breaks, to have your best year so far, to thrive, and not just survive.

Bad news may come. The economy may drop. Your health and relationships can hit hard times. The good news is that no matter what happens to us, God is still on the throne! There are no recessions in heaven. God does not cut back because of high gas prices. He's never short on food and water.

I am happy to report that all is well in His kingdom. Here is the key: As long as our Source is okay, we will be okay. If we stay connected to the vine, keeping God first, believing and expecting His favor, then as His branches we will not just survive, we will thrive!

Still, you have to keep your faith out there. Negative voices will try to steal your dreams and talk you into settling for life as it is. If you let those words take root, you will be stuck in survival mode. If you expect less, you will get less. I want you to expect more. Expect that God will increase you in a greater way. Expect this to be your best year ever!

Really, it's not that impressive to be blessed and promoted when the economy is strong, business is great, and everybody around you is being blessed. Some might say you are just benefiting from a strong economy and good times. But when times are tough and the news is dark and still God shows up and does something extraordinary—that is a great testimony to the faithfulness of our God.

When God prospers you and people see you increasing even though they're stuck, that's when they'll know it makes a difference to serve the Most High God.

Today's Prayer to *It's Your Time*

Father, thank You for the promises found in Your Word. I declare by faith that no weapon formed against me shall prosper.

Today's Thought to *It's Your Time*

As long as I keep God first, I have His favor and protection.

THE BLESSING OF GOD
FOLLOWS THE FAITHFUL

DAILY READING 2:9

Scripture Reading to *It's Your Time*   Romans 4

Even when there was no reason for hope, Abraham kept hoping—believing that he would become the father of many nations. . . .

Romans 4:18 (NLT)

Abraham and his nephew Lot moved with all of their family and all their flocks and herds to a new land. They soon realized that the land they settled was not fertile enough to support both their families with crops. Abraham, being the bigger person, told Lot, "You choose wherever you want to live and I'll go in a different direction."

Lot chose the best part of the land. He chose an area of lush green pastures, beautiful ponds, rolling hills. It looked like a postcard. Abraham was left with barren desert: rocks and sand, dry and desolate.

I'm sure at first Abraham was tempted to think, *Man, if I can just survive out here. God, how will I make it? There's not enough water, not enough supplies. How will this ever work out?*

Abraham understood this principle. He knew that as long as he was being his best, as long as He was honoring God, then wherever he went, the blessing of God went. He knew that even though he was in the desert, even though there were not enough supplies in the natural, God could still lead him to prosper—not just to survive, but to have more than enough.

It wasn't long before that desert around Abraham turned into an oasis. His crops and his herds multiplied so much, the Scripture says, that Abraham became the wealthiest man in the East.

Meanwhile, Lot was not walking in God's ways. He did not have God's favor. His land began to dry up. Abraham had to rescue Lot and his family. The story of Abraham and Lot tells me that when people do us wrong, when someone cheats you out of a promotion, someone plays politics to get the position you should have, don't worry about it. Where you are is where the blessing will be. You can be stranded on a deserted, remote island, but you will be blessed because when you arrived, the blessing arrived, too.

This is what happened to Joseph in the Scriptures. Everywhere they put him, he just kept rising to the top. His brothers threw him into a pit and then sold him into slavery to Potiphar, captain of the pharaoh's bodyguards. Potiphar put Joseph in charge of his household. Joseph was falsely accused and put in prison. The officials put him in charge of the whole prison. He stood before the pharaoh and was able to interpret his dreams. The grateful pharaoh put him in charge of the whole country.

You cannot keep a good person down. When you honor God with your life, when you're a person of excellence and integrity, you have the blessing of God. Wherever you go, just like cream, you will rise to the top. Hold your head high—not in arrogance, but in confidence knowing that wherever you go, you're taking something very special. Whether you're at work, in the grocery store, or at the ballpark, just remind yourself, *When I got here, the blessing got here!*

God wants us to be so blessed that when other people see us, they will want what we have. Back in the days when they prayed to the God of Abraham, the attitude was, "Abraham has so much favor. He's so kind, so generous, so peaceful, so blessed. If we can just reach his God we know that everything will be all right."

That's what I want people to say about you and me: "If we can just get their God, then everything will work out!"

Like Abraham, you may not be in a perfect place today. You may not have a perfect marriage, a perfect job, or a perfect neighborhood. But remember, your location does not determine the blessing. Other people don't determine your favor. God does. And the fact is, when you arrived, so did the blessing.

❧ Today's Prayer to *It's Your Time* ❧

Father, thank You for Your faithfulness in my life. I choose to put my hope in You no matter what my circumstances may look like.

❧ Today's Thought to *It's Your Time* ❧

I am blessed. Goodness and mercy are following me right now.

ALLOW YOUR HOPES TO TAKE ROOT

DAILY READING 2:10

Scripture Reading to *It's Your Time*   Job 3

What I feared has come upon me;
what I dreaded has happened to me.
Job 3:25 (NIV)

We took our son Jonathan to a restaurant when he was only a few months old. I was holding him as we ate quietly. This friendly couple came up and complimented Victoria and me on our well-behaved child. We had a nice conversation with them, but then the husband left us with this:

"You just wait till he gets to be about two years old," he warned. "It's like he'll turn into a different person. He's good now, but those terrible twos are coming."

I was tempted to say, "Thank you so much for your encouragement."

Boy, that really lifted my spirits!

Actually, I told Victoria that I refused to accept some stranger's prediction for our son.

"I am not receiving that," I said. "It will not be the terrible twos for us. It will be the terrific twos."

And I'm here to tell you that we didn't have a problem with Jonathan when he was two, or three, or four.

Then, when he was about ten years old, the naysayers started in again: "Just wait till he gets to be a teenager. He'll be giving you problems then. You'll have some headaches."

Jonathan has been a teenager for a couple years now. Do you know he still hasn't cursed or thrown tantrums? He still hasn't gotten rebellious. He's just as kind and respectful as he's always been.

Next thing people will say, "Well, just wait till he turns eighteen and gets out on his own. Wait till he hits forty. Joel, watch out because when your son gets to be seventy-five . . ."

No, I've made up my mind. I'm not activating my fears. Instead, I'm activating my faith.

We're not expecting our children to cause us problems. We're expecting them to excel. We're expecting them to do great things with their lives. Your own children will rise to the level of your expectations. If you expect them to give you trouble, cause you headaches, and not amount to much, you're allowing that to come to pass because you're putting your faith in your fears.

Do not put your faith in your fears!

Every day, all through the day, you have choices. You can believe that God is in control, believe that He's taking care of you and believe that good things are in store. Or you can go around worried, expecting the worst, wondering if you will make it.

I often hear fearful people say things like "I'm afraid I'll lose my job"; "I doubt this marriage will last"; "I just know my son will fall in with the wrong crowd."

They don't realize it, but their words show they're choosing fear over faith.

Fear and faith may seem like opposites, but they have something in common. Both ask us to believe something that we cannot see.

Fear says, "Believe the negative." *That pain in your side? That's the same thing your grandmother died from. It will probably be the end of you.*

Faith says, "Believe the positive." *That illness is not permanent. It's only temporary.*

Fear says, "Business is slow. You will go under."

Faith says, "God is supplying all of your needs."

Fear says, "You've been through too much. You'll never be happy."

Faith says, "Your best days are still out in front of you."

Here's the key: *What you meditate on takes root.* If you go around all day thinking about your fears, and you play out those fears over and over again in your mind, they will become your reality.

That's what Job warned of when he said, "What I feared has come upon me."

❧ Today's Prayer to *It's Your Time* ❧

Father, thank You for being in control of my life.

❧ Today's Thought to *It's Your Time* ❧

What I meditate on takes root.

CHOOSE FAITH OVER FEAR

DAILY READING 2:11

SCRIPTURE READING TO *IT'S YOUR TIME*   2 TIMOTHY 1

For God has not given us a spirit of fear and timidity, but of power, love, and self-discipline.
2 TIMOTHY 1:7 (NLT)

A FRIEND TOLD ME RECENTLY that everything was going great in his life. He had become engaged. His business was blessed. But instead of enjoying it, instead of thanking God for it, he said, "Joel, I'm afraid it will not last. I'm afraid it's too good to be true."

When you buy into fears, you draw in the negative. You help those fears come to pass. Negative thoughts may come to you saying things like, "You're doing well, but get ready. It will come to an end." Do not allow them to take root.

Switch over into faith and pray: "Father, You said Your favor will last for a lifetime. You said goodness and mercy will follow me all the days of my life."

None of us is immune to fear. A while back, I was facing a potentially bad situation. It had gone on for months and months. Every morning, the dread and fear hit me first thing: "This will not work out. It will cause a lot of heartache. You might as well plan for defeat."

Fear will try to dominate your thoughts. If you allow it, fear will keep you awake at night. Fear will steal your joy, steal your enthusiasm. Those fears followed me around like a dark cloud. But one day I heard God say something—not out loud, it was just an impression deep within.

He said, "Joel, if you worry about this and you keep mulling over all the reasons why it will not work out, then because of your worry, you will allow that to come to pass. But if you will trust Me and use that same energy to believe instead of worry, then I will turn around and cause it to work out to your advantage."

When I heard that, I found a new perspective. I realized that worry, fear, wrong thinking are not simply bad habits. They allow the negative to come to pass. I made a decision from that moment on: I would not worry about the bad situation anymore. When I was tempted to get discouraged, I used the temptation as a reminder to thank God that He was in control and to thank Him that He was fighting my battles for me.

✿ Today's Prayer to *It's Your Time* ✿

Father, You said Your favor will last for a lifetime. I believe goodness and mercy will follow me all the days of my life.

✿ Today's Thought to *It's Your Time* ✿

If I believe and trust in God, He will bring me out better than before.

GREAT EXPECTATIONS
MAKE FOR GREAT LIVES

DAILY READING 2:12

SCRIPTURE READING TO *IT'S YOUR TIME*   MATTHEW 9:27–34

*Then he touched their eyes and said, "According to your
faith will it be done to you";*
                                        MATTHEW 9:29 (NIV)

JESUS EXPLAINED IN MATTHEW 9:29 that we will have what our
faith expects. Too often, we expect the worst instead of believing
for the best. A friend told me about his wife, who always seemed
to think bad guys were prowling their home. At least once a week,
she'd wake him up, claiming she heard a burglar downstairs. She'd
stay on him until he'd go down and check it out every time. This
went on for years and years. Finally, one night, she did it again:
"Get up. Get up. Somebody is downstairs."

A patient man, he followed the routine just as he'd done a thousand times before. But this time, he was met at the bottom of the stairs
by a real burglar, who put a very real gun barrel between his eyes.

"Don't make a sound," the burglar said. "Just give me your
valuables."

My friend did as he was told, handing over jewelry and cash. The
burglar took the goods and was about to run off when my friend
stopped him.

"Hey, wait a minute. You can't leave yet," he said. "You should come upstairs and meet my wife. She's been expecting you for thirty years!"

Don't be like my friend's wife. Expect God's favor. I know people who are being talked into having a bad year. They've listened to the news reports so long they're expecting their finances to go down. They're expecting to barely get by. Yet their attitude should be, *I'm expecting to have my best year so far. I'm expecting God to prosper me in the desert. I'm expecting every negative situation to turn around.*

❧ Today's Prayer to *It's Your Time* ❧

Father, thank You for turning my life around.

❧ Today's Thought to *It's Your Time* ❧

I'm expecting to have my best year so far!

CHOOSE FRIENDS WHO LIFT YOU UP

DAILY READING 2:13

SCRIPTURE READING TO *IT'S YOUR TIME* PSALM 86

Give me happiness, O Lord,
for I give myself to you.
PSALM 86:4 (NLT)

PSYCHOLOGISTS DID A STUDY IN which they gave a group of people a mild electrical shock. Researchers measured their brainwaves from the time they heard they were to be shocked to the time it was over. What's interesting is they had another group in the room just watching. They measured their brainwaves as well. Even though they were not getting the shock, they experienced the same fears as those who did get jolted.

Just seeing fear in others can make us afraid, the researchers reported. A similar study found that we can catch each other's good and bad emotions just like we can catch a cold. This study at Harvard followed nearly five thousand people for more than twenty years. The researchers found that happy people pass on their good moods to others they don't even know. And those good feelings can last as long as a year.

The same study found that unhappiness can be passed on, too, but that sort of "infection" seems to be weaker than the happy version. The scientists said that a friend's happy face has more positive influence on you than a $5,000 raise. The message is that even in tough economic times, hanging out with happy friends and family members can keep your spirits high.

So if your friends are constantly complaining, talking about how bad it is and how they will not make it, my advice is to stay clear of their doom and gloom. Find some new friends. Get rid of the bad-news bears. Their worry, their fear, their discouragement are contagious. If you stay around them long enough, there's a good chance you will catch what they have.

I know you love your friends. You don't have to be rude. Don't go announce to them tomorrow morning, "Joel told me you're contagious, man. I'm staying away from you."

Please, be more tactful than that. And do me a favor. Don't use my name either.

You can be kind. You can be respectful. But gradually pull back and don't spend as much time with them and their dark moods. You shouldn't go to lunch every day with somebody who is always crying the blues and talking about how bad the economy is. You can't do that without it affecting you.

Maybe you can't always escape the doom-and-gloom crowd. Maybe a coworker is like that and you don't have a way to avoid her. Perhaps you married someone with dark moods. If that's the case, God will give you the grace to overcome. Still, when you are around depressing Debbies and gloomy Guses, make sure you take heavy doses of faith, heavy doses of hope.

❧ Today's Prayer to *It's Your Time* ❧

Father, I give myself to You and thank You for the happiness You bring to my life.

❧ Today's Thought to *It's Your Time* ❧

I will surround myself with those who lift me up.

HAVE A HAPPY HEART

DAILY READING 2:14

SCRIPTURE READING TO *IT'S YOUR TIME*   JOHN 15:9–17

> *"As the Father has loved me, so have I loved you. Now remain in my love. If you obey my commands, you will remain in my love, just as I have obeyed my Father's commands and remain in His love. I have told you this so that my joy may be in you and that your joy may be complete.*
>
> JOHN 15:9–11 (NIV)

DO YOU KNOW YOUR MOODS affect your health? Jeff, a friend of mine, found this out the hard way. His coworkers decided to play a trick on him. He went to work one morning feeling great, just as happy as can be. When he walked in, the receptionist asked, "Are you feeling okay today?"

"Yeah, I feel great," Jeff said. "Why do you ask?"

"I don't know," the receptionist replied. "You just look a little different. You look a little bit pale."

He didn't think much of her remark. He just went to his office. Ten minutes later another coworker said, "Are you real tired? You don't look up to par."

"No, I feel fine," Jeff insisted.

After a few minutes, though, he thought, *Maybe I am a little tired.*

Another coworker strolled in. They talked for a moment. Then he said, "Jeff, do you have a fever? You really look warm."

Jeff put his hand his forehead and then loosened his tie.

"You know what?" he said. "I am feeling kind of hot."

Finally, one last coworker piled on with "Jeff, you look terrible today! What's wrong with you?"

By ten in the morning Jeff was home under the covers. He was out for a week! That is the power of suggestion. If we don't guard our minds and be careful about what we allow in our brains, we can be talked into all sorts of maladies and mayhem.

Be careful: You can be talked into living a defeated life!

The formula for deep despair goes like this: Get up in the morning and turn on the television news to hear how bad things are in the world.

Next, drive to work listening to the radio with more doomsday news.

Then have lunch with the moaners and groaners in your office.

Follow that formula, and you, too, can be talked into living a defeated life. Yes, you, too, can be talked into going through life like there is a piano on your back!

Just like go-home-sick Jeff, the only thing wrong with you may be the company you keep and the sources you tune to. The television news may be mostly bad, but that does not have to be *your* reality. Sometimes the experts are wrong.

You may hear reports that "the next three years will be dreadful and disastrous." But you don't have to buy into that. You can either loosen your tie, fret, and say, "I'm feeling bad," or you can say, "You know what? I feel just great. I know God is still on the throne. He is Jehovah Jireh; the Lord my Provider. I am stronger than ever."

I'm asking you to not go home sick, let go of your dreams, settle for simply surviving because somebody talked you out of living with joy.

There is always bad news. That's one report, but we have another report. It says you are blessed. You are prosperous. You are talented. You are creative. You are well able to do what God has called you to do.

I like to watch the news. I like to know what's going on. But I'm careful to recognize when I have the information I need and when it's just redundant doom and gloom that I don't need to hear again and again.

With today's technology—twenty-four-hour cable news, the Internet, satellite radio—some days the same bleak story is told and retold a hundred different ways. Every hour it looks like a new headline, but really it's often the same old bad news repackaged.

If you are not careful, you will wear down and buy into the bleakness, the darkness, the life of just getting by. You will begin to think that it's okay to fail. It's happening to everybody.

"It's just a matter of time before I lose my house."

"I wonder when I will be laid off."

"I wonder when my health will fail."

Turn off negative talk. Fill your mind with thoughts of victory!

Just as you can be talked into having a bad year, you can be talked into having a great year. Yes, fear is contagious, but the good news is faith is *even more* contagious. Victory is viral! Joy spreads like the flu bug! That's why it's so important to get around other positive people of faith on a regular basis.

I'll give you a dose of good news: You know what's happening today? You're not catching a cold. You're catching a healing. You're not catching defeat. You're catching victory. You're not catching despair. You're catching hope. You're catching a bigger vision. You're catching God's favor.

❧ Today's Prayer to *It's Your Time* ❧

Father, thank You for filling me with Your joy as I choose love by choosing to obey Your Word.

❧ Today's Thought to *It's Your Time* ❧

I will take a daily dose of good news to maintain a joyful spirit.

THE FOG OF FEAR

—————— ❧ ——————

DAILY READING 2:15

SCRIPTURE READING TO *IT'S YOUR TIME*   ROMANS 8:12–17

> *For you did not receive a spirit that makes you a slave again to fear, but you received the Spirit of sonship. And by him we cry, "Abba, Father." The Spirit himself testifies with our spirit that we are God's children.*
>
> ROMANS 8:15–16 (NIV)

WE WERE SUPPOSED TO FLY out of Calgary, Canada, after an event, but a heavy fog rolled in. Our plane was delayed an hour or so because of it. When we finally took off I was amazed. We weren't in the air fifteen seconds before we broke through that fog. And you could look down and see it was just a small pocket of fog. It probably didn't cover more than a quarter-of-a-mile area.

Yet when we were driving to the airport and even boarding the plane, we thought the whole city was fogged in. We thought everything was shut down. But in reality it was just a tiny patch of fog.

Fear is much the same. Your fears are almost always greater than the reality. Fear feels big. It is intimidating. It will tell you: "You will never be healthy." "That child will never change." "Your finances will fall apart."

You need to face that fear and say, "You sound impressive. You look tough. But I know the truth. There's nothing really to you. You may talk a good talk, but I know your bite is not near as big as your bark. You may look permanent, but I know you're only temporary. Things in my life may be a little dark and cloudy right now. It looks like they will never change. But I have inside information. I know the sun is still shining and it's just a matter of time before this fog dissipates and the sky will be as clear and beautiful as it's always been."

When you give in to thoughts of fear, it distorts your perspective. Fear is like a fog. It obscures your vision. It makes things look worse than they really are. But it is mostly an illusion.

Do you know that a dense, hundred-foot-thick fog covering seven city blocks can be contained in less than a single full glass of water? It looks big. It looks intimidating, but, in fact, there's nothing really to it. It's just a bunch of vapors that can fit into a small glass.

Keep that in mind when fear comes creeping into your thoughts like a heavy fog, saying, "You will not make it. That sickness will be the end of you. Your marriage, your family, you will not stay together." Just look at that fear and say, "You look big. You sound impressive. But I know better. There is nothing really to you. You're just like vapor in a glass."

Your fears become more powerful when you dwell on them. You give them power by playing out every worst-case scenario as if you were watching a scary movie. Negative thoughts turn into negative images. Even small fears can become terrifying when you blow them out of proportion.

Don't let negative pictures play on the movie screen of your mind. You are the director and the audience. You are in charge. Take the remote control. Change the channel. If you let your imagination run wild, let it run wild in a positive direction.

Play the movie of you accomplishing your dreams. Show the scenes where you overcome all obstacles. See yourself healthy, prosperous, rising higher. You have to do it by faith.

❧ Today's Prayer to *It's Your Time* ❧

Father, thank You for conquering my fears and fulfilling my destiny.

❧ Today's Thought to *It's Your Time* ❧

I will not allow fear and worry into my heart.

FOLLOW YOUR VISION OF FAITH

DAILY READING 2:16

SCRIPTURE READING TO *IT'S YOUR TIME*   HEBREWS 11:1–12

Faith is the confidence that what we hope for will actually happen; it gives us assurance about things we cannot see.

HEBREWS 11:1 (NLT)

AFTER I'D BEEN MINISTERING LAKEWOOD Church for a year or so, things were going so well—the congregation was growing rapidly—that we decided to take a major step of faith and begin a second Sunday morning service. I announced in October that we would begin the new service the following January. Then, for the next few months, I was bombarded with negative thoughts questioning that big decision. *This is a big mistake. Nobody will come to the later service. You will walk out into that huge, empty church and feel like a fool.*

I did my best to stay in faith, but those fears kept playing out in my mind. Then, one night I had a dream. A better description would be a nightmare. In this dream it was that first Sunday of the new service. When I walked out to minister, there was not one person in the auditorium—not Victoria, not my mother, not one choir member, not one usher. *Nobody.*

I woke up in a cold sweat. The enemy was working overtime on my mind. He said, "Joel, there's still time to cancel the second service. You can still call it off and maybe halfway save face."

It was very difficult to get that image of an empty auditorium out of my mind. I didn't tell anybody about the dream, but I was more than a little worried about it. The week of that first service, I asked my mother, nonchalantly, if she planned on coming to the new service.

"Joel, does it start this week?" she said.

I thought, *Dear God. That nightmare might have been a prophecy.*

"Yes, it begins this week, Mother," I said. "And you need to bring your friends, cousins, relatives, casual acquaintances, and ancestors."

I had to do what I'm asking you to do. When those negative images came up, I kept changing the channel. I made up my mind. I refused to watch the Empty Auditorium Channel. I declined to tune into the Defeated News Network. I was not flipping to the *Fear Factor*. I put on a whole different show.

Through my eyes of faith I saw that second Sunday service filled to the upper deck. I kept telling myself, "This fear is just a fog. It's trying to intimidate me, but I know there is really nothing to it."

I could not wait for the new service on the first Sunday of the year 2000. I arrived an hour earlier than usual. When I pulled in, I could not believe what I saw. One parking lot was already totally full and the others were filling up fast.

There were more than six thousand people at that new service. We've been packing them in ever since!

Cast down those wrong imaginations. Do not let those negative pictures play on the movie screen of your mind. You own the remote control. Change the channel. Don't be talked into having a down year, a down month, or even a down day.

Let me talk you into having a great year. There is no obstacle too big for you, no enemy too strong. Our God is all-powerful. And you may not see better days ahead right now, but don't waste energy worrying. Plug into the highest power source and use that energy to believe in the best.

God has brought you through in the past, and He will bring you through in the future.

⤜ Today's Prayer to *It's Your Time* ⤛

Father, You've brought me through in the past, and thank You for bringing me through in the future.

⤜ Today's Thought to *It's Your Time* ⤛

I will practice discipline and control over my thoughts.

PART THREE

IT'S TIME FOR RESTORATION

GOD CONTROLS TIME

DAILY READING 3:1

SCRIPTURE READING TO *IT'S YOUR TIME*   JOEL 2:18–27

> *Then I will make up to you for the years*
> *that the swarming locust has eaten,*
> *the creeping locust,*
> *the stripping locust and the gnawing locust,*
> *my army which I sent among you.*
>
> JOEL 2:25 (NAS)

WHEN I MET LINDA AT a book signing, she told me she'd been suffering from regret over her daughter. Linda admitted that she had not been the best mother in the world. She and her daughter, Paula, had not spoken in years. She had reached out to her several times, but the daughter would not have anything to do with her.

"We lost so much time that we could have had together," she said sadly.

This mom was deeply discouraged. Linda felt she'd flunked motherhood. To my surprise that day, Linda introduced Paula standing in line behind her.

Both women had tears streaming down their faces. I didn't know what was going on, but I was getting a little teary myself.

"We had not spoken in thirteen years," Linda explained. "So

neither of us knew that we were both fans of your ministry and your books."

This divided mother and child had come separately to the book signing. They ran into each other while waiting in line and reunited that very day. When they saw each other, it was as though God had torn down the wall keeping them apart.

All the hurt, all the pain, all the resentment melted away in a split second. That night was a turning point. Their relationship was restored, and today Linda and Paula are making up for lost time!

Maybe you're dealing with a strained relationship. Maybe you've experienced conflicts and hurts. You may have built up a wall of hard feelings. You may feel someone once close to you has become a negative influence in your life.

Do not make the mistake of settling into a bitter situation. Relationships can be healed. No disagreement has to last forever. Keep believing. Keep praying.

If you will stay in faith, God will restore your relationship. And he will make up for those lost years. God wants to turn back time. We all have missed opportunities or blown chances at some time in our lives. We can look back and think, *Why didn't I put more effort into that relationship? Why didn't I take that job?* Or, *Why did I spend all those years running with the wrong crowd, partying, when I should have been getting ahead?*

Some people missed out on opportunities because they were raised in an unhealthy environment or grew up in poverty. Whatever the reason, when things don't go our way, it's tempting to think, *Too bad for me. I'll never have that chance again. I've missed my season.*

But the good news is that God always has another season. He said in the Book of Joel 2:25 that He will restore the years that have been stolen.

You may not be able to relive your childhood, but God can make the rest of your life so rewarding and so fulfilling, it makes up for lost opportunities in your past. You may feel like you've wasted years in a relationship that didn't work out, years on a job that turned out to be a dead end. Don't be discouraged.

God controls time. For every opportunity you've missed, every chance you've blown, God can turn back the clock and bring bigger and better things across your path.

❧ Today's Prayer to *It's Your Time* ❧

Father, I thank You for bigger and better things in my future.

❧ Today's Thought to *It's Your Time* ❧

If I stay in faith, God will provide another season.

GOD WILL GIVE YOU ANOTHER CHANCE

DAILY READING 3:2

SCRIPTURE READING TO *IT'S YOUR TIME*   PHILIPPIANS 3:12–17

> *I press on toward the goal to win the [supreme and heavenly] prize to which God in Christ Jesus is calling us upward.*
>
> PHILIPPIANS 3:14 (AMP)

I WAS SURPRISED WHEN A church member I'd known for a while, Riley, told me that for the first forty years of his life, he'd been a cocaine addict. He came from a good family. At one time, he was a bright young man with many opportunities, but he went astray.

"Joel, I don't even remember the first part of my life," he said. "I was so high and so messed up. I ruined my marriage. I blew my education."

At his lowest points, he thought his life was over. Yet today he is a man in his fifties with a good job and a reunited, loving family. He volunteers for us every weekend.

"I never dreamed God would give me another chance," he told me. "I never dreamed I could be this fulfilled."

What happened? God turned back time for my friend Riley. God restored those lost years. His latter days will be better than his former days. That's the way of our God.

Be bold like Hezekiah and say, "God, I'm asking You to give me back every opportunity I missed. My problems may have been my fault. I may have blown my opportunities, but God, I know You are so full of mercy. I believe You love me so much You can turn back time and give me another chance."

When you have that kind of attitude, you get God's attention. You may have given up on your dreams. You may be dragging around thinking about the years you lost in a marriage, how you were mistreated on the job, how you made poor decisions here and there.

I encourage you to reject that defeated mind-set. Don't dwell on the past. Have you ever tried to drive a car forward while looking only in the rearview mirror? You can't do that and make good progress. The same is true in life. You can't move ahead to the good if you are always looking back at the bad. Have hope. Look ahead. If you have faith, God will make up for lost time.

God says, "I control the whole universe and if I stopped the solar system for Hezekiah, I can reset the clock in your life."

If you stay in faith, a shift will occur. You may think you've blown it. You may feel you've wasted too much time. Yet I'm convinced God has new opportunities in front of you. He wants the rest of your life to be better than the first part.

God will restore the seconds, minutes, hours, days, weeks, months, and years you've lost. He will present you with opportunities you missed because you were in the wrong place. Even if it was your fault, God is so good; He's so full of mercy.

Why don't you get a vision for it? You may think that it's been too long and you've been through too much. You may have convinced yourself that you will never be able to get back those lost years. But the same God who stepped out of eternity and turned the clock back for Hezekiah says to you, "I can make up for lost time. I can restore those years."

✽ Today's Prayer to *It's Your Time* ✽

Father, today I choose to press past my circumstances and press on into You. Give me strength and hope to move forward into the life of victory You have prepared for me!

✽ Today's Thought to *It's Your Time* ✽

It's never too late to ask for God's help.

GOD PROVIDES WHAT YOU NEED

———— ❧ ————

DAILY READING 3:3

SCRIPTURE READING TO *IT'S YOUR TIME*   GENESIS 18:1–15

Then the LORD said to Abraham, "Why did Sarah laugh?
Why did she say, 'Can an old woman like me have a
baby?' Is anything too hard for the LORD? I will return
about this time next year, and Sarah will have a son."
                                        GENESIS 18:13–14 (NLT)

EVEN IF YOU HAVE ENDURED incredible hardship, keep in mind that
God can give you one idea to make up for everything that you've
lost. All you have to do is believe and be open to His blessings.

Imagine how Harland felt moving from job to job, place to
place, for many years. His father died when he was just five years
old. He dropped out of grade school and ran away from home then
bounced around, taking whatever work he could find. To make a
little extra money during the Depression, he opened a tiny restaurant, serving meals in his gas station in a small Kentucky town.

The little restaurant became so popular he had to expand to a
building across the street. Fire destroyed that place a few years
later, but Harland didn't give up. He rebuilt it. His Kentucky fried
chicken made from a secret recipe of eleven herbs and spices became so popular, the governor of the state made Harland Sanders
an honorary Kentucky colonel.

But still there was no coasting, even for the Colonel. He was in his sixties, nearing retirement age when a new highway bypass took traffic out of his little town. His business went down to nothing. He was forced to close the restaurant.

Most men his age might have given up and retired. But not Colonel Sanders. He knew God is a God of restoration. He knew God still had a way to bring his dreams to pass.

After he sold his business and paid his debts, Colonel Sanders had only $105. He hit the road, going from town to town with his chicken fryer in the back of his truck, selling his chicken to other restaurants.

Word spread quickly that Colonel Sanders's chicken was finger-lickin' good! By the time he was seventy years old, Colonel Sanders had Kentucky Fried Chicken restaurants all over the United States and Canada. Today there are more than eleven thousand KFCs all around the world. No doubt you have had a piece of Colonel Sanders's chicken. The next time you have one of his wings, think of God's restorative powers.

For a long time, life seemed to treat Harland Sanders harshly. He could easily have felt he was given the short end of the stick during those hard times. But God knows how to turn back time.

❧ Today's Prayer to *It's Your Time* ❧

Father, I know that for You all things are possible.

❧ Today's Thought to *It's Your Time* ❧

Nothing is too hard for the Lord!

GOD WILL NOT GIVE YOU MORE THAN YOU CAN HANDLE

DAILY READING 3:4

<small>SCRIPTURE READING TO</small> *IT'S YOUR TIME*   <small>GENESIS</small> 50:14–21

You intended to harm me, but God intended it all for good. . . .

<small>GENESIS</small> 50:20 (NLT)

I HEARD A FUNNY STORY about Farmer Jacob, who had a mule named Caesar that fell into an abandoned well fifty feet deep. Jacob really loved this old mule. But when he surveyed the situation, he realized there was no way to rescue old Caesar.

The well was very narrow and Caesar was crammed at the bottom. The mule had not moved or made a sound. Jacob figured Caesar died in the fall. As much as it bothered him to give up on the mule, he was a practical farmer. He decided to leave Caesar at the bottom of the well and fill it up with dirt.

Jacob called some friends to help shovel dirt down the well. The first shovel load of dirt woke up Caesar, who'd been knocked out. When the mule felt the next load of dirt hit his back, he realized what was going on. But instead of letting himself be buried, Caesar shook it off.

Every time a load of dirt hit his back, the mule shook his body, tossing the dirt to his hooves. Then he'd step out of it.

Caesar kept it up. Shake and step. Shake and step.

After nearly an hour of shoveling dirt, Farmer Jacob and his helpers were stunned to see Caesar's ears appear at the top of the well. They realized that the mule was not dead. So they kept shoveling until the old mule stepped out of the well and walked to freedom.

They'd come to bury Caesar, but they raised him instead! When you feel the dirt hit your back, when life treats you unfairly, when you go through disappointments, don't let it bury you. Shake it off and step up.

As that wise mule figured out, the same dirt that could bury you also could be your salvation. In your case, it contains the seeds of your rebirth sent by God to promote you. Your attitude should be "I may be down, but I'm not staying down. This difficulty was meant to destroy me. It was meant to harm me, but I know better. God is using it to my advantage. He's using it to increase me."

If you have a big challenge today, that just means you have a big destiny. Extraordinary people face extraordinary difficulties. But the good news is we serve an extraordinary God. He has you in the palm of His hand.

In tough times you've got to draw the line in the sand. Make a declaration: "This difficulty will not bury me. This loss, this disappointment, this injustice, will not cause me to give up on my dreams. I refuse to live in self-pity. I know I am a seed. That means I cannot be buried. I can only be planted. I may be down, but it's only temporary. I'm not only coming back; I will come back better off than I was before."

✣ Today's Prayer to *It's Your Time* ✣

Father, thank You for keeping me in the palm of Your hand.

✣ Today's Thought to *It's Your Time* ✣

I refuse to live in self-pity. I am a seed who can be planted but not buried.

GOD MAKES UP FOR LOST TIME

DAILY READING 3:5

SCRIPTURE READING TO *IT'S YOUR TIME*   2 CORINTHIANS 12:1–9

Concerning this thing I pleaded with the Lord three times that it might depart me. And He said to me, "My grace is sufficient for you, for My strength is made perfect in weakness." Therefore most gladly I will rather boast in my infirmities, that the power of Christ may rest upon me.

2 CORINTHIANS 12:8–9 (NKJV)

OUR DAUGHTER ALEXANDRA WAS BORN a month and a half before my father went to be with the Lord. During that time my dad was on dialysis for his failing kidneys, and often I would take him up to the clinic and bring him home. It was a very busy season in my life.

Then, when Dad died I was thrust into serving as pastor. I was doing my best just to stay above water. Looking back, I can hardly remember the first couple years of Alexandra's life. It was such a time of transition. I was swept up in learning how to minister, trying to figure out everything.

The new role just consumed me. One day not long ago, I was struck by the fact that I don't have as many memories of Alexandra's early childhood as I do of her brother Jonathan's. It bothered me, so I prayed on it, almost in passing. I said, "God, I'm asking You to make up for that lost time when I was so busy and so preoccupied with other things."

Today, I feel Alexandra and I are as close as we can be. She likes to do everything with her dad. She would rather do cartwheels in the backyard for me than visit with her friends. It warms my heart. We're so close I even tease her that sometimes I need a break from her.

"Alexandra, don't you want to go to your cousins'?" I'll say, kidding. "You all can go swimming or something. Why don't you have some friends over?"

"No, Daddy," she'll play along, "I just want to stay here with you."

I believe we have bonded so closely thanks to God turning back the clock and making up for those lost years.

You may feel as though you weren't as good a parent as you should have been. You were busy doing your own thing, dealing with your own issues. Maybe now your relationships with your family are not what they should be. You're tempted to feel guilty and think, *If I had just spent more time with them, if I'd of just made them a higher priority.* Instead of giving in to guilt, do something far more constructive. Ask God, as I did, for another chance.

✣ Today's Prayer to *It's Your Time* ✣

God, restore this relationship. Let me put into it the time, effort, and feeling required to heal it. Anything I missed, I'm asking You to allow me to make up for lost time.

✣ Today's Thought to *It's Your Time* ✣

My God is a God of second chances.

STAY ON THE HIGH ROAD

———— ✍ ————

DAILY READING 3:6

SCRIPTURE READING TO *IT'S YOUR TIME* 1 SAMUEL 25:23–38

*Please forgive me if I have offended you in any way. The
LORD will surely reward you with a lasting dynasty, for
you are fighting the LORD's battles. And you have not
done wrong throughout your entire life.*

1 SAMUEL 25:28 (NLT)

At one point, King David had an *I don't care* attitude. Out of
frustration, he was about to make a foolish decision and attack
Nabel and his family. David was on edge. It was taking so long for
him to see God's promise come to pass. He knew he was destined
to take the throne, but years had gone by and it hadn't happened.

Nabel's wife, Abigail, stepped up and reminded David of his
destiny. She convinced him not to attack her family. "David, why
would you even bother with my husband?" she said. "You are the
next king of Israel. That would be like swatting a fly."

She spoke sense into David, reminding him of God's promise over his life. I believe God sends us an Abigail any time we
are about to delay our divine destiny. When you are tempted
to be frustrated, you must keep God's promises in the forefront
of your mind. Down deep you have dreams and desires; you
know one day you will accomplish your goals. One day you will

be well. One day you will be out of debt. One day you will be vindicated.

Maybe right now things don't look so good. Like David, maybe you are in one of those wilderness periods. You don't see anything positive happening. It is very tempting to think, *What's the use? It will never change. I've been believing for five, ten, fifteen years.*

Let me serve as the voice of Abigail: Stay the course. Keep believing. You may be tired, discouraged, and frustrated but don't give up on your future. It may be taking a long time, but stay focused. Stay on the high road and keep being your best.

I wasn't there when God spoke the promise to you. But I believe what God has said about you. You can overcome every obstacle. You can break every addiction. You can live an abundant life. I believe new seasons of favor and increase are coming your way. I know God can restore the years. He can turn back time. Don't give up on your future.

You may have been through heartache and pain. You have had disappointments and unfairness in your life. But the depth of your past foretells the height of your future. When a skyscraper is to be constructed high into the sky, the builders must first dig low to give it a solid foundation. Only then can the structure rise to its full height. Your foundation is being formed. It may be taking a long time, but if you'll stay in faith, God is preparing you. Don't let your guard down, don't compromise your future. You have too much to lose.

God is saying to you, "If you will persevere even though it's difficult and believe even though you don't see anything happening, then I will step in and do what you can't do. I will make up for lost time. I will propel you to new levels. I will bring supernatural opportunities. I will open new doors. I will put the right people in your path. I will heal the sick. I will release you from debt and lack. The chains of addictions and wrong thinking will be broken off of you."

God says, "The promises I put in you, I will bring them to pass."

Why don't you get a vision for that today? God will make up for your lost time. Every opportunity you've missed, every chance you've blown, all those years you may have wasted, I declare over you; restoration is coming your way.

God will restore those years. Things are changing in your favor. Your latter days will be better than your former days. I declare the rest of your life will be better than the first part of your life. So receive it by faith!

✤ Today's Prayer to *It's Your Time* ✤

Father, thank You for stepping in and doing what I cannot do.

✤ Today's Thought to *It's Your Time* ✤

If I persevere, God will bring His promises to pass.

DON'T TALK ABOUT PROBLEMS, TALK ABOUT YOUR GOD

DAILY READING 3:7

SCRIPTURE READING TO *IT'S YOUR TIME*   PSALM 68:1–10

> *Rise up, O God, and scatter your enemies.*
> *Let those who hate God run for their lives.*
>   PSALM 68:1 (NLT)

WHEN YOU LET GOD ARISE in your life and you show unshakeable confidence, you are like the farmer waiting for harvest. You know that it will be better than expected. You know down deep that nothing can defeat you. No one can keep you from your destiny. Every setback is only temporary.

Instead of complaining, you say, "I can't wait to see what God will do." When you let God arise, you might as well get ready. Your enemies—sickness, debt, depression, disappointment—will be scattered; none of those enemies can stay.

Let me ask you today, "What are you letting arise? What are you lifting up?"

You may be dealing with hard times—you lost your job, your retirement fund was cut in half, stress has made you sick, your relationships have suffered.

But you can't focus on what happened to you. If you do that, you are letting the wrong things arise. That's defeat, discouragement, self-pity. You need to turn it around and say, "God is still in control. I may be hurting right now, but I know God will bring better days. God is the Restorer of my soul. He's giving me beauty for my ashes.

"I know God is my provider. He is supplying all of my needs.

"God is my Vindicator. He will make my wrongs right. He is fighting my battles."

When you let God arise, you can't stay defeated. Your enemies will be scattered. As a young man, Moses had a desire to deliver the people of Israel, but he strayed from God's path and he killed a man. He had to run for his life. He spent forty years on the back side of the desert. It looked like he was buried. It looked like his dreams would never come to pass. The truth is, he wasn't buried. He was simply planted. He was coming back. Those dreams were still alive. During all those years out in the wilderness Moses didn't get bitter. He didn't get discouraged. He knew God was still in control. One day when Moses was eighty years old, God came and said, "Moses, it's time for your comeback. It's time for you to blossom. I've got an assignment for you."

Do you know the latter part of Moses's life was much greater than the first part? You may feel like Moses, like you've made too many mistakes and missed too many opportunities.

But God wants the rest of your life to be the most fulfilling, the most rewarding. Those dreams that you once had, they didn't die. They're still alive on the inside. You may have made poor choices, but they didn't bury you. They planted you. God has already arranged your comeback. Now you need to do your part and get your fire back.

Quit living condemned. Quit listening to the accuser reminding you of everything you've done wrong. God knew every mistake you would ever make. The moment you asked Him for forgiveness, He forgave you. And the good news is, He didn't cancel your destiny. He didn't give away your assignment. You need to stand tall and say, "That's it. I'm not living condemned anymore. If God gave Moses another chance, He'll give me another chance. This is a new day."

You've been created to overcome every obstacle, to rise above every challenge. I want you to have confidence so that no matter what comes against you, it cannot defeat you. As long as you're letting God arise, your enemies will be scattered.

❧ Today's Prayer to *It's Your Time* ❧

Father, I can't wait to see what You do! I worship You and praise Your holy name.

❧ Today's Thought to *It's Your Time* ❧

This is the day I'm putting on a new attitude.

BE A BOUNCE-BACK PERSON

SCRIPTURE READING TO *IT'S YOUR TIME*   PSALM 92

But the godly will flourish like palm trees
and grow strong like the cedars of Lebanon.
                    PSALM 92:12 (NLT)

AFTER HURRICANE IKE ROARED THROUGH Houston, we lost many huge oak trees, some of them four or five feet around. Those trees, which had looked as sturdy as can be, were no match for the 100-mile-an-hour winds.

I saw pine trees 140 feet tall knocked down in yard after yard. Big trees, small trees, pines, oaks, elms, magnolias were brought down. None of them could withstand those hurricane-force winds.

There was just one type of tree that seemed to fare better than most others in this powerful storm—the skinny, flimsy palm tree. Do you know why palms held up so well?

God designed the palm tree to bend but not break in high winds. The palm tree can bend all the way over until its top touches the ground and still not break. Palms may be bent over for four or five hours during a strong hurricane. You'd think they would snap right off, as thin as they are, but palms are resilient. They bounce right back.

I can imagine Hurricane Ike huffing and puffing and thinking, *I may not be able to uproot you, but at least I will keep you from ever standing up again.* That hurricane just kept blowing. Old Ike thought he'd blown those palms off their roots. But when the hurricane ran out of steam, when Ike's winds died down, the palms bounced back!

After the storm, the palms around Houston just rose up, fanned out their fronds, took a deep breath, and said, "Well, that was a nice breeze. Hey, where'd all the oaks and magnolias go?"

Why is that? God built resilience into the palm tree. It may get bent over by the forces of Nature, but it is only a matter of time before the palm stands tall once again. Palm trees don't sweat storms. They weather them. During Hurricane Ike, our palm trees were not worried. They weren't depressed or thinking, *Oh, no. Another hurricane. This will be the one. I'm sure it will tear me up by the roots.*

Our palms were at peace. Our other trees were going down left and right, but the palm takes pride in its resilience. Palms know Almighty God put bounce in their bark.

I learned something even more amazing about palms. Biologists say that during a hurricane when the palm tree is being bent and pushed over, its root system is actually strengthened by the stress, which gives it new opportunities for growth.

When the storm is over, the palm tree smiles and says, "I knew this would be a bad one. I knew I would be battered. But what do you know? I came back up stronger than I was before. Now, if you will excuse me, I think I'll grow a little taller."

That's what God says will happen to each of us, if we just stay in faith. Psalm 92:12 says, "The righteous man will flourish like the palm tree."

Isn't that interesting? God could have said we would flourish like the mighty oak trees—big, sturdy, with great branches. Or God might have said we'd flourish like pine trees—tall and majestic, able to see for miles!

But God chose palm trees because He knew there would be difficult times in which we would have to bend so we wouldn't break. He knew things would come against us, trying to steal our joy, our victory. So God said, "You will be like a palm tree, because I've put a bounce back in your spirit."

The storms of life will come. The winds will blow. At times, it might look like you're finished, like it's all over for you. You might get a bad report about your health. You might be passed over for a promotion or laid off. Other times, it might appear that your dream has died. But just like that palm tree, when the storm is over, you will not stay down. You will bounce back and keep growing.

We all face disappointments and setbacks. But the key is to develop a bounce-back mentality.

When you get knocked down, don't stay down. Get up to fight another day. Disappointments hit. Disruptions happen. But pity parties are not the answer.

God has promised that what was meant to harm you, He will use for your good.

When you're resilient, you know that every adversity, every setback is only temporary. It will not last forever. Weeping may endure for a night, but you know joy is coming in the morning. So you don't sit around complaining, thinking about how bad it was and everything you've lost.

God is a God of restoration. He has promised to pay you back double for every unfair situation. Instead of being discouraged by the difficulty, you are encouraged by challenges because you know you will receive double for your trouble! Yes, despite your challenges today, tomorrow you will come out better off than you were before.

❧ Today's Prayer to *It's Your Time* ❧

Father, I will stay in faith so that whatever was meant to stop me will become a stepping-stone instead.

❧ Today's Thought to *It's Your Time* ❧

I will bend with hard times and then grow.

GET YOUR HOPES UP

DAILY READING 3:9

SCRIPTURE READING TO *IT'S YOUR TIME*   PROVERBS 24:1–22

The godly may trip seven times, but they will get up again.
But one disaster is enough to overthrow the wicked.
                                    PROVERBS 24:16 (NLT)

PROVERBS 24:16 SAYS THAT A good person may fall seven times, yet the Lord will raise him up. One of my staff members has a family member, Chris, who had three battles with cancer before his fortieth birthday. His most recent fight was the worst. They found a tumor wrapped around his spine. Things looked dark for Chris, who is married with three young children. But Chris is one of those upbeat people who bend without breaking. His favorite shirts have a logo that says: *Life is good!*

Chris was knocked down and laid low by a deadly disease that third time. Because of the tumor's location, chemotherapy was not an option. He prayed, and every night for inspiration he read my mother's book on surviving cancer.

Then one day, Chris got an unexpected call from a major cancer center. Doctors there said that his previous fights with cancer qualified him for a special, experimental program. He was given a new test drug that targets only cancer cells.

The experimental drug wiped out the tumor without making Chris the least bit sick. He's healthy again. *Life is good!*

Ill winds may be blowing in your own life today. Dark clouds may be hovering. Maybe you too have a health issue, maybe your job was downsized, maybe one of your family members has gone astray.

Your attitude should be, "It's just a matter of time before this turns around. This sickness may have me down, but I'm not staying down. God is restoring health back to me. Life is good!"

Times may be tough. The storm may be raging. But your faith will allow you to bend without breaking. You are righteous. You do your best to please God. When this storm is over, you will not be broken or flat on the ground. You will not be defeated or depressed. You will be stronger, healthier, increased, and promoted!

Today's Prayer to *It's Your Time*

Father, thank You for creating me to live in victory. I am more than a conqueror through You.

Today's Thought to *It's Your Time*

I am a child of the Most High God!

GOD WATCHES OVER HIS CHILDREN

DAILY READING 3:10

SCRIPTURE READING TO *IT'S YOUR TIME*   ISAIAH 59

> *So shall they fear the name of the LORD from the west,
> and his glory from the rising of the sun. When the enemy
> shall come in like a flood, the Spirit of the LORD shall
> lift up a standard against him.*
>
> ISAIAH 59:19 (KJV)

He holds us in the palm of His hand. God knows every struggle, every lonely night, every unfair situation. A little sparrow cannot fall to the ground without God knowing about it. How much more is God concerned about you and me, His sons and daughters? The Scripture says, "When the enemy comes in like a flood . . ." That means when you feel overwhelmed, when the hurricane hits, and the stock market dips, what does God do?

He doesn't say, "Too bad. I told you life was hard. You should have made better decisions." No, when the enemy comes in like a flood, God raises up a barrier. In other words, that gets God's attention. He does not sit back and make us fight our battles on our own. That's when God steps up to turn things in our favor.

When you see a child in trouble, you don't think twice. You just naturally stop what you are doing and go to help the child in need. When our son Jonathan was about two years old, we were in the grocery store with him. I'd left him with the cart as I strolled down to the end of the aisle. I was only about forty or fifty feet away. I could still see him. But while I was looking for something, he knocked a few cereal boxes off the bottom shelves, making a little mess. It was no big deal. But this employee came around the corner and lost it. She jumped down Jonathan's throat.

"Listen here, young man," she scolded. "You need to learn to keep your hands to yourself. And you may not make a mess in this store."

On and on she went, letting my son have it beyond anything he deserved.

Something rose up in me. I don't know if it was God or the devil. But it sure felt good. I consider myself a nice person. I'm kind. I'm friendly. I'll help anybody with anything. But when somebody messes with my children, that is a different story.

I don't know if you've ever seen the Incredible Hulk, but mild-mannered Pastor Joel had a little of the Hulk going on that day. One minute, I was this normal-looking guy in the cereal section. Then, all of a sudden I underwent this superhero transformation. No, my shirt didn't rip apart from bulging muscles. My skin did not turn green. But that's how I felt! I was ready to take on a tiger.

You can mess with me. You can say, "Joel is too this, too that." No big deal. It doesn't bother me. It bounces off me. But if you mess with my children, you've got Pastor Hulk on your hands!

I may not be big and green, but dynamite comes in small packages.

Our Heavenly Father is the same way when it comes to protecting His children. When the enemy wades in on the attack, whether he sends sickness to attack your body, somebody to mistreat you, or the wrong things to happen despite your effort to do right, whatever the challenge, God doesn't sit back and say, "Too bad."

No, God steps up and says, "Hey, you're messing with the wrong person. That's My child. That's My son. That's My daughter. If you mess with them, you are messing with Me. And who am I? Well, I am the all-powerful Creator of the universe."

God looks at your enemies and says in effect, "You want some of this? Go ahead and make my day." God says, "I am your protection. I am your deliverer. I am your healer. I am your strength. I am your wisdom. I am your victory."

You are not alone. In the toughest of times, you've got backup, way up! Almighty God has your back. He's got a hedge of protection around you, a bloodline that the enemy cannot cross. Nothing you are going through can keep you from your God-given destiny. You have bounced back before and you will do it again. You may be a little bent because of the strong winds, but the good news is you're not broke and you will bounce back again.

I love the way David put it: "God lifted me out of the horrible pit . . . and put a new song in my mouth."

God will lift you in the same way. Where you are now is not where you will always be. There are brighter days up ahead. Favor, promotion, increase; no good thing will God withhold because you walk uprightly.

Still, remember you must do your part. Put a new song in your heart. Sing the song of victory. If somebody asks you how you're doing, don't give them a detailed report of every ache, pain, leak, and overdue bill.

Your attitude should be, "I'm too blessed to be stressed. I'm healthy. My family is well. *Life is good.*"

Finally, remember that each setback offers the time to plan a comeback. In the middle of the adversity, in the middle of the tough time, you need to start making your list of who you will invite to your victory celebration.

✤ Today's Prayer to *It's Your Time* ✤

Father, thank You for lifting me up and putting a new song in my heart.

✤ Today's Thought to *It's Your Time* ✤

I'm too blessed to be stressed. Life is good!

LIVE A RESURRECTED LIFE

DAILY READING 3:11

SCRIPTURE READING TO *IT'S YOUR TIME*   ISAIAH 61

> *To appoint unto them that mourn in Zion, to give unto them beauty for ashes, the oil of joy for mourning, the garment of praise for the spirit of heaviness; that they might be called trees of righteousness, the planting of the LORD, that he might be glorified.*
>
> ISAIAH 61:3 (KJV)

JESUS ENDURED PAIN ON THE cross by focusing on the joy set before Him. What are you focusing on today, what didn't work out? Who hurt you? How unfair it was? Or, are you focusing on your dreams and your goals, knowing that your best days are still in front of you?

Even though adversities may look like stumbling blocks, God can use them as stepping-stones to take you to a higher level. Everything you've gone through in life—every adversity, every lonely time—God was doing something on the inside. He is preparing you.

You wouldn't be who you are today. You wouldn't have the depth, the maturity, the insight were it not for those challenges that forced you to grow. Keep your life in a positive perspective. We are not defined by our pasts. You are not defined by how you were raised, or by how you were treated, or even by the mistakes you've made.

So shake off self-pity. Shake off bitterness. Shake off hurt. You may have seen one of your dreams die. Maybe you lost a job, your savings, or a loved one. But failures and losses are part of life, not the end of it. Jesus died, was buried, and then rose again. That is how God works. You've been through death. You've been through the burial. Now it is the third day. It is time for your resurrection.

If you want to live a resurrected life, you must have a resurrected mentality. In other words: "I may have been cheated in a business deal, but I'm not bitter. I'm not sour. I know that didn't happen *to* me. That happened *for* me. God said He would be my vindicator. God said He would pay me back double for every injustice. So I will not drag around defeated. I will stay in faith knowing that the hard times just qualified me for double the blessings."

Maybe you've been dealing with poor health for a long time. Your medical report doesn't look good. You could be down and discouraged. But instead, tell yourself, "I know this isn't happening *to* me. It's happening *for* me. God is in complete control. And I believe He will turn it around, He will make me better off than I was before."

Maybe you've made poor choices. You've made some mistakes and opened the door to trouble. Now comes the condemning voice. The accuser tells you, "You blew it. It's your fault. You can't expect anything good."

No, you've got to shake that off and say, "I may have brought trouble upon myself, but I know God's mercy is bigger than any mistakes I've made. I will not live with guilt. I will not give up on my dreams. I know I'm growing. I'm learning. And in the end, God will use it all to my advantage."

Develop this resurrection mentality. You are a child of the Most High God. Nothing can happen to you. It can only happen for you. It's all a part of God's plan. You may feel that none of your dreams have come to pass. That simply means you've been through the death. You've been through the burial. Now it's time for restoration. The good news is that it's not over until God says it's over.

He still can bring your dreams to pass. Why don't you get in agreement with Him? Reject the victim mentality. When you have the right perspective, you take away all the power of the enemy. When things turn against you, in the natural, you may get down and discouraged. You may complain and feel defeated.

But you need to understand that eventually God will create good out of it. Even though your life may be difficult now, God is depositing something on the inside. Once you understand that, you can wear a smile even when your plans don't work out. You can be at peace even when you should be stressed out.

You may have a boss, a friend, a child who is difficult to get along with. Sometimes you have to look at difficult people and just say it in faith: "You are not happening to me. You are happening for me." They may not understand it, but don't bother explaining it to them.

This may seem funny, but I need to thank some of my enemies. I need to write them a check. They don't realize how God has used them to stretch me, to grow me, to help me have greater confidence in Him. When we were trying to acquire the Compaq Center in Houston for our church, one of the major business leaders in the city told a friend of mine, "It will be a cold day in Hell before Lakewood ever gets the Compaq Center."

That man doesn't know what he did for me. I should buy him dinner (McDonald's, probably). I don't know if we would have one of the country's largest churches today if it were not for him. God used him to light a new fire on the inside, to give me a new determination, a new passion. He didn't happen to me. He happened for me.

At first I was thinking, *Wow. We've got a lot of things coming against us. It looks like our opponents are very big, very powerful.* But I had to shake that off and say, "No. If God be for us, who dare be against us? The bigger they are, the harder they fall."

Too many times people give up on their dreams without a fight. They stop believing. I've seen people miss out on God's best because they never move beyond the burial stage. They are hit with a disappointment and instead of burying it and knowing that God has another plan, instead of getting a fresh vision for their life, they wallow in self-pity.

You will never reach your resurrection, you will never enter phase three if you don't keep going beyond the death and the burial. You must have the attitude *I did my best; I gave it my all.*

❦ Today's Prayer to *It's Your Time* ❦

Father, I'm preparing myself for the new things You will do in my life.

❦ Today's Thought to *It's Your Time* ❦

I can be good to people even when they are not good to me.

ENCOURAGE YOURSELF

DAILY READING 3:12

SCRIPTURE READING TO *IT'S YOUR TIME*   PSALM 84:6

Passing through the Valley of Weeping (Baca), they make it a place of springs; the early rain also fills [the pools] with blessings.

PSALM 84:6 (AMP)

A PASTOR FRIEND TOLD ME about a man in his congregation who was always complaining, always in need. My friend finally got tired of it. He prayed, "God, would you just move this man to another church? He is draining all my strength and energy, taking all my time."

The pastor told me he heard God speak to him deep down inside. God said to him, "I won't move him from your church. That man has kept you on your knees praying like nothing I've ever seen before!"

It's not happening to you. It's happening for you.

The fact is, we grow in difficult times. That's when character is developed. Yes, it's fun to be on the mountaintop where it's easy but you are not being stretched. Growth comes when you have to overlook an insult, forgive a wrong, and do the right thing even when the wrong thing is happening.

I'm not saying anyone should ask for tough times. But when they come my way I've already made up my mind that I will not grow sour. I'll not be bitter. I'll be better. I'll know God is trying to deposit something on the inside.

I love what David said: "Though I walk through the valley of the shadow of death . . ." He didn't say, "Though I live in the valley." Or "Though I'm stuck in the valley." Or "Though I'll probably die in the valley."

No, he described this valley as *temporary*. He said, *"I will not die with these problems. This too shall pass."* The fact is, everyone faces challenges at some point, whether you have health problems, financial difficulties, or a struggling relationship. We all have something in the natural that could steal our joy and cause us to be worried. But we've got to keep things in perspective, like David, and say, "No, I'm going *through* this. This didn't come to stay. It came to pass."

If you are dealing with a challenge, you need to remind yourself all through the day, "This is temporary. I may be lonely right now, but I will not stay lonely. I know God will bring the right person into my life."

Or "I may be wounded emotionally. I may be hurting on the inside. But I will not stay wounded. I know God is the restorer of my soul. He will bring healing and give me beauty for these ashes."

Encourage yourself. Don't settle in the valley of darkness. That is not your permanent address.

You'll look up and think, *I should be down. I should be stressed out. I have so much working against me. But I'm happy. I'm at peace. I'm expecting good things.*

Why is that? It's because you're tapping into those pools of blessings and God is refreshing you.

I know sometimes when you go through loss, it is easy to feel like you have been robbed. Maybe you lost a loved one, a marriage; maybe your childhood was unhappy because of a bad environment. When you experience a loss, you can have one of two attitudes. You can say, "God, this isn't fair. Why did this happen? It doesn't make any sense." You can be bitter and negative, and live with anger in your heart.

But a much better approach is to take that loss and sow it as a seed. Just say, "God, I don't really know why this has happened to me. I don't know why this has been taken away. But God, I will not allow anyone or anything to steal from me. I'm giving it to You as a seed, trusting that You will bring me a harvest."

Maybe you lost your job in the recession. Just say, "God, nobody stole my job from me. I know You control the whole universe. And even though it wasn't right, God, I'm giving it to You as a seed trusting that You will bring me an even better job."

❧ Today's Prayer to *It's Your Time* ❧

Father, I believe that You will bring me divine connections, that You will guide the right people into my life.

❧ Today's Thought to *It's Your Time* ❧

I will turn my life over to God for the harvest He can bring.

GOD ALWAYS HAS THE FINAL SAY

DAILY READING 3:13

Scripture Reading to *It's Your Time*   Psalm 1

They are like trees planted along the riverbank,
bearing fruit each season.
Their leaves never wither,
and they prosper in all they do.

Psalm 1:3 (NLT)

Before Jesus came to the Resurrection He endured the Garden of Gethsemane, the road to Golgotha, and death on the Cross. Those were His biggest challenges. And they lead to His greatest moment. Many times on the way to our dreams being fulfilled, we go through these same types of experiences.

When Jesus prayed for Peter, He didn't pray that he would never have to deal with challenges. He prayed that His faith would remain strong. In the Garden of Gethsemane, Jesus was so distraught over what He was about to face. He was in such agony in His spirit that He sweated great drops of blood. He said, "Father, if You're willing, take this cup from me. Nevertheless, not My will, Yours be done."

It was there in the garden that Jesus made a decision to hold on to the promise that God put in His heart. There, deep inside, a war was under way. Everything within Him was telling Jesus, "I will not make it. There's no way. It's too tough." But when Jesus made the decision to stay in faith, God sent an angel to strengthen Him.

You may feel like you're in the garden right now. It may seem that the world has turned against you. You cannot seem to find a way through your hard times in the natural. But God is saying, "Hold on to that promise. Keep believing. Keep hoping. Keep praying. You are close to your victory."

On the road to His crucifixion, Jesus was forced to carry His own cross. But He had been so beaten down, so mistreated, He couldn't carry it the whole way. He fell under the weight of His cross. The message is that you don't have to be strong 100 percent of the time.

Sometimes the weight of your burdens will force you to your knees. Do not despair. The accusing voice will tell you that you are not strong enough if every day is not a perfect day, if you don't stay in faith every minute, if you don't keep your joy and peace at all times.

Yet remember that even Jesus fell under the weight of His cross. Simon came to his aid. He helped Jesus carry His burden. God also will send someone to be there for you in your time of greatest need.

Maybe today it's my voice lifting you: "You can make it. There are better days up ahead."

But the enemy will try to hold you down: "You had a bad day. You had a pity party. You lost your temper. You yelled at your kids."

God wants to ease your burden. He is saying, "That's okay. You're human. I know what it feels like to fall down. I've been there. Just get back up again. You've got a resurrection coming."

They nailed Jesus to the cross. And as He hung there He felt so lonely, so dejected, He cried out, "My God, My God. Why have You forsaken Me?"

Jesus asked a question, but He didn't hear an answer. Sometimes Heaven can be silent. You pray. You believe you are doing your best, but you don't see anything happening. You're hurting on the inside. Your life may appear to be over. But in those silent times something powerful is happening deep inside. God is stretching you. You're developing a greater confidence in Him.

Your mind may tell you, "It's over. My dream will never happen." But something will rise up in your spirit that says, "No, God is still on the throne. This is not happening *to* me. It's happening *for* me. And even though it doesn't seem fair, even though I'm discouraged, deep down I know my resurrection is coming. I know God can still turn this around."

As Jesus hung on the cross in all that pain, the soldiers made fun of Him. They mocked and ridiculed Him. Yet in spite of all His suffering, in spite of the disrespect, He looked up to Heaven and said, "Father, forgive them. They don't know what they are doing."

Jesus forgave His enemies. Then he committed His spirit into His Father's hands. They put Him in the grave. I'm sure the forces of darkness were celebrating, rejoicing, thinking they had finally won the victory. But they didn't realize it's not over until God says it's over.

God controls the universe. Jesus was buried on Friday. Three days later, on Sunday morning, He rose from His grave.

"I am He that lives," Jesus said. "I was dead, but I am alive forevermore. Because I live, you can live also."

Today's Prayer to *It's Your Time*

Father, help me to grow and to be strong in my faith.

Today's Thought to *It's Your Time*

God always has the final say!

FOCUS ON YOUR "RIGHT NOW" GOALS

DAILY READING 3:14

SCRIPTURE READING TO *IT'S YOUR TIME*   JOHN 11:1–44

Everyone who lives in me and believes in me will never ever die. Do you believe this, Martha?"

JOHN 11:26 (NLT)

GOD HAS AN ABUNDANT LIFE in store for each one of us. But many times on the way to your victories, just like Jesus, you will experience setbacks and difficult times. Remind yourself, "It's not happening to me. It's happening for me. God is preparing me. On the inside He is depositing strength, courage, and ability."

You must have a "now" mentality. Do not fall into the "one day" mentality: "One day I will be happy"; "One day God will work in my life."

Now is the time to release your faith. *Right now*, God is working in your life. *Right now*, God is arranging things in your favor. *Right now*, God is filling you with His strength.

Stay in the now. That's what activates God's power.

When Mary and Martha arrived at the tomb of their brother Lazarus, he had been dead four days. They were crying and so distraught. Then Jesus appeared and said, "I am the Resurrection and the life."

"Yes, Jesus," the women said, "we know in the last days You

will raise our brother Lazarus from the dead when we all go to Heaven."

Jesus said in effect, "No, Mary. No, Martha. I'm not talking about in the last days. I'm talking about *today*. If you'll roll away the stone, I will raise your brother right now."

Jesus was saying, "I am a *right now* God."

Often, we settle into that *one day* frame of mind: "One day God will do something great in my life"; "One day God will resurrect my dead dreams."

Break free of that mentality. Believe that *today* God will do something great. *Today* God will open supernatural doors. Have a *now* mentality.

You may have been through the death, so to speak. You've been through the burial. You've been hurt, disappointed, discouraged, or downed by sickness or heartbreak. But God didn't take you through those challenges just to leave you beaten down, bedraggled, or half dead.

"Well, how you doing, brother?"

"Oh, pretty good under the circumstances."

No, it's time for your resurrection. It's time for you to rise up and take everything that belongs to you. If you've been crucified with Christ, you can be raised with Christ. The enemy may have done his best, but his best will never be enough.

Shake off the past. Shake off every disappointment. Shake off every injustice. Shake off every failure. Let today be a new beginning. You may feel like you're in the garden, down and discouraged. But take heart. Your resurrection is coming. You may have fallen under the weight of your cross. God is saying, "Get back up. You're close to your victory."

You may even feel like you're on the cross: Your dreams have died. Everything is coming against you. But you must take a new perspective. Nothing in life has happened to you. It has happened for you.

God will take what was meant to destroy you and use it to thrust you into your divine destiny. Remember, you are not defined by your past. You are prepared by your past. Every adversity, every obstacle is God depositing something on the inside.

If you'll live this resurrected life, you will live in victory. Even when things come against you, you'll still have a smile on your face. You'll know God is not only turning your life around, He is giving you beauty for ashes, joy for mourning, and in the end you will come out stronger, happier, healthier—better off than you were before.

✥ Today's Prayer to *It's Your Time* ✥

Father, thank You for hearing me when I pray to You.

✥ Today's Thought to *It's Your Time* ✥

I will stay in faith and live in victory.

SUNDAY IS COMING

DAILY READING 3:15

SCRIPTURE READING TO *IT'S YOUR TIME*   LUKE 18:31–42

> *They will flog Him and kill Him; and on the third day
> He will rise again.*
>
> LUKE 18:33 (AMP)

WHENEVER WE DISCUSS THE RESURRECTION of Christ, I think about when they crucified Jesus on that dark Friday. It was the most painful, discouraging day of His life. In fact, it was so bad, earlier Jesus sweated great drops of blood.

It looked like His days were over. Most thought His enemies had the best of Him. But God had other plans. They put the body of Jesus in the grave on Friday and they celebrated their victory.

But Sunday morning was a different story.

The grave could not hold Him. Death could not contain Him. The forces of darkness could not stop Him. On the third day Jesus came out of the grave and He said, "I was dead, but now I am alive forevermore."

One principle the Resurrection teaches us is that God will always finish what He started. No matter how dark it looks, no matter how long it's been, no matter how many people are trying to push us down, if we stay in faith, God will take us from Friday to Sunday. He will complete the plan He created for you.

You may feel like it's a Friday in your life right now. The economic downturn has hurt so many people. For some already struggling, it has added more stress, more burdens.

You may have major obstacles in your path. You can't see how you will ever accomplish your dreams, or how you can recover your health, or resolve your problems. Negative thoughts are bombarding you: *It's over. Just accept it. It will never be any better.*

It may feel like Friday, but my encouragement is, *Sunday is coming.* God is a faithful God. The promises He put in your heart—that you will be healthy, that you're coming out of debt, that your family will be restored, that you'll have a supernatural year—God has every intention of bringing them to pass. He is called the Author and the Finisher of our faith. God will never begin something without finishing it.

When God put the dream in your heart—a dream to start a business, to find a better job, to be in ministry—the good news is that He already has a completion date. God can already see it done. You may not see how it can happen. It may be taking a long time. All the odds appear to be against you. But if you'll just keep believing, keep praying, keep being your best, then God promises to complete His plan for you.

He will take you from Friday to Sunday. Your children may have served God when they were younger, but now they've gotten off course. They're not doing what is right. Well, God is saying, "Get ready. They're coming back." It may be today. It may be next month. It may be next year. But it will happen. God finishes what He starts.

Maybe you have a dream to get out of debt, to pay off your house, to be free from that burden, but it looks impossible. The economy is down. Business is slow. You've gone as far as your education allows.

But God is saying, "I'm not limited by those things. I've got resurrection power. I can give you one break that will thrust you to a new level. I can open doors that no man can shut. I can bring talent out of you that you didn't know you had. I can send people who will go out of their way to be good to you."

Keep believing and you will come into supernatural increase. Maybe you're single and have a desire to meet somebody. You've been through a couple of relationships that didn't work out. Now it's been a long time. Your thoughts are telling you, *You're never going to meet anybody. You're washed up. You had your chance.*

No. God is saying, "I've already picked out the right person. I'm lining up things in your favor. I'm causing you to be at the right place at the right time. You will see that promise come to fulfillment."

Is there something that once excited you? Are there dreams you've abandoned? Goals you've let go? If a dream has taken too long and disappointments have made us complacent, we sometimes accept that "It's probably not going to happen for me."

The first place we lose the battle is in our minds. You may think, *I could never start that business, Joel; I don't get any good breaks. I could never get a new house; I can't even sell my old house. I'll never go back to college; I don't have the funds.*

Just because you gave up on your dream doesn't mean God gave up on you. The dream He put in your heart may be buried under disappointments, setbacks, failures, and rejections. But know this: The seed is still alive. The promise is still in you.

Fan that flame. Get your fire back. It may look like your dream is dead, but the fact is it's not buried. It's planted. That means it's coming back!

Your attitude should be, "This may take a long time. I had some bad breaks. I don't see how it could happen. But I know God already has the completion date. So I won't give up on my dreams. I'm not going through life with no goals, no enthusiasm, no passion. No, I'm getting my vision back. I'm greeting every morning with great expectations. It may be Friday, but this I know: Sunday is coming."

Today's Prayer to *It's Your Time*

Father, thank You for Your resurrection power. I choose to keep my eyes on You, the Author and Finisher of my faith.

Today's Thought to *It's Your Time*

God never abandons a dream.

WHAT LOOKS LIKE THE END
IS ONLY THE BEGINNING

DAILY READING 3:16

Scripture Reading to *It's Your Time* Philippians 1:3–11

In all my prayers for all of you, I always pray with joy because of your partnership in the gospel from the first day until now, being confident of this, that he who began a good work in you will carry it on to completion until the day of Christ Jesus.

Philippians 1:4–6 (NIV)

The last thing Jesus said on the cross was, "It is finished." It certainly looked like the end. It looked like it was over. But I believe that wasn't just a statement of fact. It was a statement of faith. He was saying to His Father, "I've done my part. I've fulfilled my destiny. Now I've got total trust and confidence in You. I know that You will finish what You started."

When your path seems darkest and you feel lost and defeated, dare to make a declaration of faith just like Jesus: "It is finished."

What you're really saying is, "God, I know You will turn this situation around. I know You will heal my body. I know You will restore my family. I know You will give me the breaks I need."

Don't complain. Speak victory over your circumstances. If you have a contract to close and the deal is falling apart, say, "Father, thank You, it is finished. This house will sell. This agreement will go through. This new client will be mine."

If you have the burden of heavy debt, you need to announce to that debt, "It is finished." Look at that house payment. "It is finished." Look at that college loan. "It is finished." Look at those unpaid bills. "It is finished."

A young American couple began doing missionary work in Mexico in the 1960s. Their dream was to help the less fortunate, to bring God's message of hope to the Mexican people. So they left behind the comforts of home to raise their three small boys in a foreign land.

One Sunday while they were here in the States visiting family, the missionary family came to a service at Lakewood Church. My father's church was very small back then, just a couple hundred people. The missionaries met my parents before the service and talked for a moment. Then, during that service my dad told a little of their story. At the end he received an offering for this young couple.

His Lakewood congregation gave this couple a check for $600. They were so excited, so appreciative. They went back to Mexico and used that money to start a Bible school. Tragically, the husband was killed two years later when his small plane crashed while he was taking Bibles to rural areas of Mexico.

As you can imagine, it was a dark day for his wife and their children. It was definitely a dark Friday in their lives. It looked as though her dreams had died. She was a twenty-four-year-old widow raising three boys under the age of four. This young woman could have easily come back to the States and given up on the dream of helping poor Mexican people. No one would have blamed her.

But she didn't do that. She understood this principle: She knew that God always finishes what He starts. She knew that even though it was a dark Friday, a better Sunday was coming—just as it does on Easter week each year in church.

So she stayed there and continued on with the Mexican Bible school. And something interesting happened. Over time, she noticed that one of her sons had an incredible gift for music. He could sing, play the piano. He had a natural gift of communication.

That boy, Marcos Witt, grew up to be the Spanish pastor at Lakewood. He has done great things, touching many lives here and across Latin America. He fills huge stadiums for his concerts. He's won multiple Grammy Awards.

What happened? *Sunday came.* God completed what He had begun.

Philippians 1:6 tells us to be confident of this; He that began a good work in you will bring it to completion. Notice we're supposed to *be confident*. Talk like it's a sure thing. Act like it is a done deal. Plan like it's already happened.

Not any of this: "My son will never straighten up. The more I pray, the worse he gets."

No, be confident: "Yes, he's making poor choices right now, but I know he will turn around. I know it's just a matter of time before he is back on the right track."

That's confidence. That's your faith speaking.

Be confident by saying, "I know God will bring somebody great into my life. I can't wait to meet up."

Marcos's mother, Nola, had a dream to touch her community. But now because Sunday came, through her son, she's touching the whole world. God didn't just complete the promise, He brought Nola out to a *flourishing finish*.

❧ Today's Prayer to *It's Your Time* ❧

Father, thank You for allowing faith to rise in my heart so I, too, might come to a flourishing finish.

❧ Today's Thought to *It's Your Time* ❧

If I get into agreement with God, He will do more for me than I can ask.

YOURS IS A GOD OF COMPLETION

---❦---

DAILY READING 3:17

Scripture Reading to *It's Your Time*   2 Kings 13:14–21

> *Once when some Israelites were burying a man, they spied a band of these raiders. So they hastily threw the corpse into the tomb of Elisha and fled. But as soon as the body touched Elisha's bones, the dead man revived and jumped to his feet!*
>
> 2 Kings 13:21 (NLT)

In the Scripture, there are seven major miracles attributed to Elijah, who was promised a "double portion" of Elijah's anointing. That meant Elisha should have experienced fourteen miracles. Yet Elisha found himself on his deathbed after experiencing only thirteen miracles. He was one short of the promised allotment! With that in mind, Elisha probably hoped that reports of his impending death were exaggerated. After all, He knew that God is a God of completion.

Still, God works according to His own plan. With just thirteen miracles on his record, Elisha died! His surprised family then placed him in an open grave. I wonder if they chiseled on his tombstone: "One miracle short."

Elisha's body was still in the open grave when along came a group of people carrying a man killed in battle. They were in a hurry, so they decided to put his body in with Elisha's. They lowered him in and when his body touched Elisha's, the prophet came back to life. He stood up and walked out of that grave!

I can imagine his friends took off running when they saw that. Still, there was miracle number fourteen! God came through when it counted the most. And that tells me that as long as we stay in faith, as long as we keep believing, every promise God's put in our hearts will come to pass. Not even death can keep God from bringing it to completion.

This brings a whole new meaning to the phrase "Hang in there!" There are many similar accounts in the Bible. Consider, for example, Zerubbabel from the Old Testament. God had put in him a desire to rebuild the temple on Mount Moriah in a city that had been destroyed. Zerubbabel built the foundation of that temple, but people who lived nearby stopped him from doing any more work.

For ten years there was no progress on the temple. I'm sure Zerubbabel must have thought, *God, I started out so well. I laid the foundation. I had these big dreams. But people came against me and I could not finish the job.* You can imagine how discouraged he must have been, but then, after ten years had passed, a prophet by the name of Zechariah came by. He said, "Zerubbabel, God sent me all this way to give you two words: *Start again.*"

With those words, Zerubbabel's faith was stirred. I can imagine him thinking, *You mean God can still bring this to pass? Don't you know it has been ten years? Do you know how many people are against me? Do you really think I can do this?*

Zechariah said, "I don't think you can do it. I know you can do it."

I believe God says the same thing to you. "Start again. Get your dreams back. Get your hopes up."

You may have wanted to buy a new house, but you didn't qualify. Try again.

Maybe at one time you believed you could overcome an addiction, but it's been so long that you've accepted where you are. God says, "Try again."

Maybe you had a dream to do something great, but you had disappointments. Your family didn't get behind you. Nobody encouraged you and now you think it could never happen. God says, "Start again."

After a decade, Zerubbabel started again. Zechariah then instructed him to bring out the capstone, which is the final piece of stone set aside to mark completion of the temple. It was important to keep the capstone on display as the work continued, because every time he looked at it, Zerubbabel was reminded that God is a God of completion.

When Zerubbabel was tired, when he was down, when he thought it was impossible, he'd go back over and look at the capstone and be reminded of God's promise to complete His plan.

⚜ Today's Prayer to *It's Your Time* ⚜

Father, I have faith that every promise You put in my heart will come to pass.

⚜ Today's Thought to *It's Your Time* ⚜

Even when things look dark, I need to remember that God will bring His plan to completion.

YOU CAN TRUST GOD
WITH YOUR DREAMS

DAILY READING 3:18

Scripture Reading to *It's Your Time*   Psalm 106:40–46

He remembered his covenant with them
and relented because of his unfailing love.
Psalm 106:45 (NLT)

From the time he was a boy, my brother, Paul, had a desire to serve on medical missions in Africa. He'd journeyed to Africa at the age of twelve on a mission with my father, and that trip made a lasting impression on him. He returned to Africa as a college student to work with underprivileged people. He vowed that he would return to be of more help once he obtained his medical degree.

His dream was delayed, but on God's good time. For seventeen years, Paul was a surgeon in Arkansas, working his way up to chief of surgery at a hospital. Yet even with all of that success, he and my sister-in-law, Jennifer, had this powerful desire to serve as medical missionaries.

At one time or another, they applied to various mission groups. But none of those efforts bore fruit. Usually the timing wasn't right, some other responsibility came up, so their dream was delayed.

Then, last year a group of doctors from our ministry planned a trip to Africa. They invited Paul to go. He had moved back to Houston in 1999 to help us pastor our father's church. If Paul hadn't made that move, he might not have been in a position to go to Africa.

He joined the doctors on the mission to Africa, where he performed surgery in a small clinic. Paul found the missionary work so rewarding that he came back home, rounded up his family, and took them to Africa for three months more. Near the end of that mission, Paul stood outdoors one night, looked up at the beautiful African sky, and was overwhelmed with gratitude. Finally, he was living his dream. He was doing exactly what God put in his heart as a little boy. God brought that promise to pass.

If you feel your dream has been delayed, know that God has a plan. Be patient. My brother first felt that call to Africa at the age of twelve. That desire was only heightened by another visit ten years later. Yet it was more than twenty years before he truly lived the dream.

You may never have shared your dream with anyone, yet God knows. He put those desires in your heart. You do your part. He will do His. You should do your best every day. Pursue excellence. Live with integrity. Treat others with respect and kindness. Every day that you live as a good Christian brings you closer to the fulfillment of God's promise.

Patience is critical. Psalm 106 warns that the people of Israel missed their promise because they became discouraged. They complained and gave up hope. Don't let that happen to you. Stay in faith. Recognize that God may be testing you. If you let His plan unfold, you'll find that God will give you something better than you dreamed.

On the dark Fridays of your life, when things aren't going your way, remind yourself that the light of Sunday is coming. Your own resurrection is on its way. Be confident of that.

The promise God placed in your heart is alive and well. Live with that expectancy. Believe and declare that you will see your dreams and promises come to pass, and they will be better than you expected. God will bring you to a flourishing finish; it's time for restoration.

❧ Today's Prayer to *It's Your Time* ❧

Father, thank You for helping me exceed my expectations with Your guidance.

❧ Today's Thought to *It's Your Time* ❧

Every day that I live in faith brings me closer to the fulfillment of God's promise.

PART FOUR

IT'S TIME TO TRUST

ALL THINGS WORK TOGETHER FOR OUR GOOD

DAILY READING 4:1

Scripture Reading to *It's Your Time*   Romans 8:18–30

*And we know that God causes all things to work to-
gether for good to those who love God, to those who are
called according to His purpose.*
                                                                Romans 8:28 (NAS)

A CHURCH MEMBER STOPPED ME the other day and told me he'd
lost his job of many years. He didn't understand why this had
happened to him. "I gave that company my best. I was loyal. I was
always there on time. It was just not right," he said.

I told him although life is not always fair, God is fair. The Scripture says that God causes all things to work together for our good.
The key word is *together*. You cannot isolate one part of your life
and think, *This is not good. It's not good that I got laid off. It's not
good that my loved one got sick. It is not good that my relationship
did not work out.*

That in itself is not good. But God can see the big picture. That
disappointment is not the end. Your life doesn't stop because you
got a bad break. That is simply one part of the puzzle. There will
be another piece that connects it all. It will work together for your
good.

When my children were younger, we loved to make chocolate chip cookies. We baked together so often, we didn't need the recipe. We knew exactly what to do. Each of us had a role: Jonathan was in charge of the brown sugar and the eggs. Alexandra was our flour, baking soda, and vanilla person. And I was the bowl and mixer man.

We were very precise cookie makers. We always put in exactly the same amount in the same order. We used two bowls because at one point, we mixed the contents of the smaller bowl into the larger bowl. We beat in one egg at a time. We'd learned that to make the best-tasting cookies we had to follow our special family recipe down to the last chocolate chip.

Once, we forgot to put in the baking soda. I thought it was no big deal since we used only a teaspoon of it. "How could that matter in such a large bowl?" But those cookies came out of the oven flat as could be. They weren't chocolate chips. They were chocolate chunks. They didn't rise one bit. They were thick as wood chips. Nobody would eat them.

What was the problem with this batch of cookies? We left out a key ingredient. Though just a spoonful was missing, it made a huge difference.

Some people are bitter about life because they haven't waited for all of the ingredients to come together. God has promised a great plan for you. He has predestined you to live in victory.

When bad things happen, you might not understand the purpose. You may not understand why you lost your job, why you became ill, why your relationship hit the rocks. Don't get stuck there. God has more ingredients coming your way.

It's time to trust.

You may feel your life is flat today: flat finances, flat career, flat marriage. But all God has to do is add His own heavenly baking soda and your life will rise to a new level.

You may have seen chef Emeril Lagasse on television. When he adds an ingredient, he always says, "Bam!"

Just imagine God putting a little more favor in your life—*Bam!* A healing—*Bam!* A good break—*Bam!*

Maybe you are lonely. All God has to do is mix in the missing ingredient—a divine connection. *Bam!*

Maybe you're at odds with a child. God adds a pinch of supernatural restoration. *Bam!*

I don't know about you, but I'm expecting some "Bams!" in my life. I'm expecting God to come up with the right ingredients: the right people, the right opportunities, the right breaks at just the right time.

You may have had some disappointments. Life may not have treated you fairly. But you would not be alive if God was not planning another victory in your future. That setback was not the end. That breakup you went through years ago may not have made sense, but there is another ingredient coming. God will pull it all together.

Your life may not seem exciting or maybe you are not seeing much growth. That's because your chocolate chips haven't been mixed in yet. Don't be discouraged. You don't know what God has in mind for you.

❧ Today's Prayer to *It's Your Time* ❧

Father, thank You for planning a victory in my future.

❧ Today's Thought to *It's Your Time* ❧

With just a few more ingredients, God will sweeten my life!

STAY OPEN TO GOD'S PLAN

DAILY READING 4:2

SCRIPTURE READING TO *IT'S YOUR TIME*   PROVERBS 22–36

> *Joyful are those who listen to me,*
> *watching for me daily at my gates,*
> *waiting for me outside my home!*
> PROVERBS 8:34 (NLT)

SCOTT WAS GIVEN UP FOR adoption at six weeks of age. When he turned two, he developed a mysterious illness that stunted his growth. At first, doctors thought his illness might be cystic fibrosis, but they ruled that out. For six years Scott was in and out of the hospitals. Doctors could not figure out what was hindering his growth.

Eventually, he got a little better and started growing, but he was still very small. His dream in school was to play sports—baseball, basketball, football—but he was too small. To make matters worse, some of the kids bullied him, made fun of him, and called him names. It didn't look like God had a plan. Scott's life didn't seem to make sense. But remember, it's not over until God says it's over. All Scott needed was a few more ingredients.

He'd been given up by his parents, and that sort of rejection is hard enough to deal with. He spent years in and out of the hospital, and that, too, would be very discouraging. But setbacks and hard times are not permanent. Life goes on. As long as you are here, there is always more to the mix.

Sooner or later, God adds His special ingredients. He blends in a spoonful of His favor, a cup of His goodness, and then sprinkles in a few of His supernatural breaks. Then all of a sudden, a bitter life turns sweet.

Scott never did become a star in basketball, baseball, or football. He didn't have the physical size for those sports. Still, he had his own special gifts and when he found the right mix, he became a great athlete.

Scott knew God didn't make mistakes. When he realized he would always be too small for other sports, he laced on his ice skates and went to lessons with his sister. It wasn't long before the coach noticed Scott was an extremely gifted skater. In fact, he was Olympic caliber! Still, some experts told him he was too small even for that sport: "You don't have a chance. You're just wasting your time."

But Scott already had learned how to deal with adversity. He'd grown up faced with challenges. Adversity was nothing new to him. His early challenges had prepared him for later victories.

You are not who others say you are. You are who God says you are. God said Scott Hamilton was a victor. This small man with a big heart won every national and international skating championship for four straight years, including the 1984 Olympic gold medal.

In the natural, you may not see how you can accomplish your goals. You cannot understand what God has put in your heart. But know that all of your ingredients are not in the mix yet.

❧ Today's Prayer to *It's Your Time* ❧

Father, help me to keep moving closer to experiencing Your victory in my life.

❧ Today's Thought to *It's Your Time* ❧

If I follow the Lord's lead, He will open supernatural opportunities for me.

EVEN BITTER WATERS
CAN CARRY A BLESSING

DAILY READING 4:3

SCRIPTURE READING TO *IT'S YOUR TIME*   JOB 13:1–19

Why do I put myself in jeopardy
and take my life in my hands?
Though he slay me, yet will I hope in him;
I will surely defend my ways to his face.

Indeed, this will turn out for my deliverance,
for no godless man would dare come before him!
                              JOB 13:14–16 (NIV)

NANCY BRINKER WAS JUST THREE years older than her lively little sister, Suzy. Nancy was more serious, more career-oriented, but they were always close. Even as adults living in different cities, they talked every day on the telephone. One day, Suzy told Nancy that she'd been diagnosed with breast cancer. Nancy immediately flew to be with her. She went with Suzy for treatments in Houston and other cities. She stayed by her side through nine operations in six months.

After fighting together for three years, Nancy lost Suzy. It was a bitter blow. Yet Nancy was determined that her sister's death would make the world a better place. No doubt, you have seen the results of Nancy's determined efforts. She created the Susan G. Komen Breast Cancer Foundation, which has raised more than $1 billion for cancer research through its Race for the Cure events. It is the world's largest grassroots network for breast cancer survivors and activists. Much good has come from Nancy's grief for her beloved little sister.

The symbol for the word *crisis* in Chinese is made up of two words: *danger* and *opportunity*. In every crisis, in every loss, in every disappointment there is the danger of growing bitter, staying bitter, settling for less. Yet there is also always the opportunity to turn darkness into light just as Nancy Brinker did.

We can grow. We can step out in faith. We can stretch ourselves to experience the new things that God has in store. You may not have the time and resources to launch a national organization like Nancy Brinker did, but you can make a difference in your own neighborhood, community, or congregation.

I was reminded of this while speaking with Wes and Val Herndon from our church. They are fine and faithful people who lost their teenage daughter Katy to cancer. We prayed and believed with them for many, many years as she battled the disease. Katy held on to life as long as she possibly could, but then she went home to the Lord.

As you can imagine, her grieving parents tasted some bitter waters. They didn't know why their daughter had to die. Even though it was difficult, they committed her passing into God's hands. Today, the Herndons serve as shining examples of how God can turn your life around. They radiate God's goodness. Whenever I meet someone grieving the loss of a child, I think of this couple. I often put them in touch with others going through grief.

They went through a major crisis. I can't think of anything bigger. They faced the darkness. They could easily be negative, bitter, angry people, blaming God, asking, "Why did this happen?"

But in their crisis they saw the opportunity. They saw a chance to receive God's grace. Today the Herndons are helping others to make it through.

God wants to show His grace through you.

When you go through a crisis, instead of becoming bitter, believe that God is still in control. Stay hopeful and believe that He will open new opportunities, and then you, too, will become an example of God's amazing grace. You not only will see God's goodness in a greater way, but you will inspire others to keep moving forward into the good things God has in store.

I love the way Job put it: "Though He slay me, yet will I trust in Him." Job had this unwavering trust because he knew God was still on the throne. When we go through things that don't make sense, things that we don't understand, we should call to mind Job and his faith: "I'm not worried about it. I know God is still in complete control of my life. I know He has me in the palm of His hand. This may look like the end, but I know God has a new beginning. Weeping may endure for a night, but I know a secret: Joy is coming in the morning!"

✑ Today's Prayer to *It's Your Time* ✑

Thank You, Father, for being in complete control of my life. You have me in the palm of Your hand.

✑ Today's Thought to *It's Your Time* ✑

My weeping may endure for a night but I know a secret: Joy is coming in the morning!

YOUR MESS MAY BE YOUR MESSAGE

DAILY READING 4:4

SCRIPTURE READING FOR *IT'S YOUR TIME*   ISAIAH 40:12–31

> *but those who hope in the LORD*
> *will renew their strength.*
> *They will soar on wings like eagles;*
> *they will run and not grow weary,*
> *they will walk and not be faint.*
>
> ISAIAH 40:31 (NIV)

I READ ABOUT A YOUNG woman whose father underwent a heart transplant. Though at first he seemed to be doing well, several months later he died. She was in another city, working on her master's degree, when she learned of his passing. She packed and went to the airport to catch the first flight to her father's town.

She was so upset, so heartbroken. While waiting for her flight, her grief overcame her. She wept uncontrollably. She did not see the man come up, but she felt these loving arms around her and then she heard a voice saying, "Ma'am, what's wrong?"

She recognized the voice. She looked up and it was Kevin Costner, the actor and director. Struck by her sadness, he had stopped to offer this stranger his help. She explained that her father had passed away. The actor comforted her, staying with her so long he missed his own flight.

As he walked her to her boarding gate, Costner mentioned that he would be returning to her city to film a movie. He asked her to stop by and let him know how she was doing. Several months later, she was driving in heavy traffic near her home. She realized the backup was caused by a movie crew working in a nearby park. She wondered if it was Kevin Costner's movie, but then she thought she should not interrupt even if it was.

Later in the day, she drove by the same spot. This time, something compelled her to stop. She learned that it was Costner's movie. She told a security guard that he had invited her to stop by. He took her to meet Costner. The Academy Award winner was just as kind and warm to her as he had been at the airport. He invited her to watch the scene being filmed.

After a few minutes, an executive in charge of the production came and sat next to the young lady, just being friendly. He explained the scene being filmed and the role of each crew member. She found it easy to talk with him. Soon, they were bantering like old friends.

That night, she called her mother and said, "Today I met the man of my dreams. I'm going to marry him."

Sure enough, they began dating, fell in love, and one year later, they were married. Who would have thought that crying in an airport would turn out to be a significant piece of her puzzle? God used that moment like a connecting piece, to connect her with her future husband.

That is an amazing story, I know. But we have an amazing Father in Heaven. God has the pieces to the puzzle of your life. Because it is incomplete, that puzzle may not make sense right now. Don't get discouraged. There is another piece coming. This one will complete you.

God has some more in store for you. He will turn your mourning into dancing. He will lift you out of mediocrity into a life of fulfillment.

Keep dreaming. Stay in faith. Play it out in your mind. Learn to shake off bitterness. Do not dwell on unanswered questions. Believe that God is in complete control. He will transform your scars into stars. He will make your mess into your message.

❧ Today's Prayer to *It's Your Time* ❧

Father, I know that You will put together all the pieces and make me whole.

❧ Today's Thought to *It's Your Time* ❧

God will show up and show out in unusual ways.

GOD REMEMBERS YOU

DAILY READING 4:5

SCRIPTURE READING TO *IT'S YOUR TIME*   PSALM 115

The LORD remembers us and will bless us . . .
PSALM 115:12 (NLT)

LAKEWOOD'S SINGERS WERE LEADING WORSHIP during a church service several years ago when I looked out over the congregation and a thought struck me. I didn't see my niece Savannah. My sister April's seven-year-old was staying at our house that weekend. She was supposed to be at the service with us.

I leaned over to Victoria and asked, "Where is Savannah sitting?"

"I don't know," Victoria said. "Where did you put her?"

"I didn't put her anywhere," I said. "I didn't bring her. You brought her."

Victoria's eyes grew even bigger than usual.

"No, Joel. I thought you brought her."

My heart sank.

Victoria and I usually drive separately to church on Sunday because I need to get there earlier. I thought she was bringing Savannah. Apparently, she thought I'd brought her.

We'd left my little niece at home all by herself!

Crazy thoughts raced through my mind. I had just watched the movie *Home Alone*. I envisioned Savannah wandering through the house hollering and screaming.

She could be scarred for life! I thought.

I was up on the platform in the middle of a service with thousands of people. I was trying to look spiritual, trying to appear holy. But on the inside I was in a total panic.

Headlines flashed before my eyes: "Pastor Arrested for Leaving Child at Home!"

We were thirty minutes from home. Victoria and I debated whether to call the police or a neighbor. Finally, we decided to call my brother-in-law, Kevin, who lives just a few minutes from us. As soon as we told him, he ran to our house. He found little Savannah sitting at the back door just as peaceful as can be.

With a sweet smile on her face, she was not the least bit worried, not the least bit upset. The first thing she said to Kevin was, "I knew you would remember me."

Later, I asked if she wasn't just a little scared.

"No, Uncle Jo-Jo," she replied sweetly. "I knew you would come back for me."

If only we could all have that same childlike faith when we feel forgotten and alone, when things aren't going our way. If, instead of getting negative, bitter, or into self-pity, we could just shake off those negative feelings and say like little Savannah did, "I'm not worried. I know God remembers me. I know it's just a matter of time before He shows up and turns it around."

I don't think it's an accident that the phrase "God remembers you" is found seventy-three times in the Scripture. He wants us to know He's there for us. "God remembers you" means more than God has not forgotten you. It's more significant than that. When we're told, *God remembers you*, it means He will overwhelm us with His favor. He will surprise us with His goodness.

❧ Today's Prayer to *It's Your Time* ❧

Father, thank You for your overwhelming favor each and every day.

❧ Today's Thought to *It's Your Time* ❧

God remembers me and it's just a matter of time before He shows up in my life.

GOD'S GREAT PROMISE

DAILY READING 4:6

SCRIPTURE READING TO *IT'S YOUR TIME*   ISAIAH 49:8–26

See, I have engraved you on the palms of my hands;
your walls are ever before me.

ISAIAH 49:16 (NIV)

AFTER A CHURCH SERVICE ONE day, a man told me, "Joel, I've been praying about a situation for years, but I don't see anything happening."

He felt forgotten.

Another member of our church told me she had been in an abusive relationship that left her feeling as though "I don't matter anymore."

She was so beaten down, she couldn't even look at me.

Have you ever felt like those hurting people? Have you ever prayed and prayed, but it seemed like God was on vacation? Have you ever had those seasons when everybody around you was being blessed, but the good breaks just passed you by? You felt overlooked. Even though you were in a relationship, or married, you still felt all alone?

Do you have a smile on the outside but feel empty on the inside? Do you feel as though nobody knows what you are going through and, worse, nobody cares?

I know it is easy to feel forgotten. But when loneliness sets in, look to God's great promise. *You are not forgotten. You are not abandoned. God remembers you!*

You may have been sick for years, feeling like your health will never change for the better. But God knows every sick and lonely night. He sees every tear you've ever shed. He has you carved into the palm of His hand.

Maybe you have a dream in your heart, but every time you reach for it, you come up short. *I'll never do this. It will never happen.*

God has not forgotten about you. In fact, even right now He's working in your life, arranging the right people, the right breaks, the right opportunities. So, at just the right time, in your due season, you will see that dream come to fulfillment!

Maybe you're a parent. You're raising your children. You're making all kinds of sacrifices so their dreams can come to pass. But know this: God has not forgotten about your own dreams. He has not forgotten about the personal goals put on hold for your children. He sees your sacrifices. He's saying, "Not only will I help your children succeed, I will help you fulfill the desires of your own heart."

I want you to get your hopes up today. Put your shoulders back. Hold your head up high. People may forget you, but God will never forget about you. Others may do you wrong. Friends may betray you. Those you count on may leave you when you need them the most, but God is the friend who sticks closer than a brother.

When life deals you a tough blow, when you pray, but the heavens are silent, when it's taking longer than you think, you need to remind yourself of this promise: "God has not forgotten about me. He has not forgotten about my hopes and dreams. He's not forgotten about the unfair things I've been through. He's not forgotten about my years of sacrificing, my years of giving, my years of serving."

It's just a matter of time before you reap your harvest for the seeds you've sown.

Remember Nat "King" Cole's signature song "Unforgettable"? You are just as unforgettable to our God. You matter to Him. He has carved you into the palm of His hand. When God looks at you, all He can say is, "That's my masterpiece. That child makes me proud. That person brings a smile to my face. That is the one who brings joy to My spirit."

✑ Today's Prayer to *It's Your Time* ✑

Father, thank You for keeping me in Your heart and on Your path.

✑ Today's Thought to *It's Your Time* ✑

I will not drag through life negative, defeated, feeling alone, left out, forgotten. I know God remembers me.

GOD WILL MAKE YOU FRUITFUL

DAILY READING 4:7

SCRIPTURE READING TO *IT'S YOUR TIME*   GENESIS 41:37–57

> *Joseph named his firstborn Manasseh and said, "It is because God has made me forget all my trouble and all my father's household." The second son he named Ephraim and said, "It is because God has made me fruitful in the land of my suffering."*
>
> GENESIS 41:51–52 (NIV)

I MET A WOMAN WHO'D come to Houston for cancer treatment at the big medical center. She was from a smaller city. She was very nervous about the treatment to begin with, and then she also was intimidated about being in a large city all by herself for three months, she told me.

The first couple of weeks she felt so alone, nobody to talk to, like she had been forgotten. She said she always watched our services on television, so her dream was to come to one at our church. But she didn't have a ride and she didn't know anybody who could give her one. She had special medical needs that made it difficult to travel without help.

But one day in the hospital cafeteria line, she overheard the couple behind her talking about attending services at Lakewood each weekend. She told them she enjoyed watching the services on television.

The couple offered right away to bring her to a service.

"We'll come by and pick you up this Sunday," they said.

Their offer was a dream come true. She was thrilled. They brought her into our church and as she walked in, all she could do was weep and weep. The greeters gave her a hug at the door. When she said she was a first-time visitor, they brought her down and sat her in the very front row.

She was so excited. She told me afterward, "Joel, I sat right by your brother Paul."

I apologized.

"You're right," she said. "He's not near as good looking as you are."

Okay, she didn't say that, but I know she was thinking it.

No, what she was really thinking was that God had remembered her. He had sent the right people to the right place to let her know she was not forgotten. Better yet, the Lakewood members she'd met at the hospital offered to bring her to services every Sunday as long as she was in town. She attended our services for three months.

She was not forgotten. My friend, neither are you!

In the Bible, Joseph was betrayed by his brothers. He was falsely accused by a lady and spent thirteen years in prison for something he didn't do. I'm sure he must have felt, "God has forgotten about me. Look how my life has turned out. I thought I had a dream. I thought I had a promise. I must have been wrong."

Yet the story of Joseph also teaches us that we should see hard times as a test of faith. When things aren't going our way, we have the opportunity to find out what we are made of. What kind of attitude will we have? Will we be negative, bitter? Will we blame God? Or will we stay in faith knowing that God has us in the palm of His hand?

Joseph used his gift for interpreting dreams to help his cell mates. He told one, the pharaoh's butler, that he would be freed in three days' time. Then, Joseph asked the butler to put in a good word for him with the pharaoh when he left. Sure enough, the butler was released three days later. But wouldn't you know it? He forgot all about Joseph.

Sometimes the people who owe you the most will forget you the quickest. But don't worry. Don't get discouraged. Just because they forgot about you doesn't mean God has abandoned you.

When Joseph was released later, he was promoted. I love what he said: "What was meant for my harm, God used to my advantage." When you're faced with difficulties that never seem to end, keep reminding yourself, "God has not forgotten me."

Many hardworking people have dealt with foreclosures on their homes in recent years. I read about one woman who was laid off and couldn't make her payments. The bank foreclosed and put her home up for auction with several others. She had already accepted that it was over, that a chapter in her life was through. She was doing her best to deal with it, but down deep she was heartbroken.

A single mother, she had raised her children in that home. I'm sure she felt like Rachel: alone, forgotten, like nobody really cared. Here goes her house that meant so much to her. Just to get closure, she went to the bank's big auction of all its foreclosed homes. There, all she could do was weep and weep seeing not just her house but her home on the auction block.

A lady noticed her weeping, came up, and asked her what was going on. She explained that she'd lost her job and now her home was about to be sold. The lady showed her the list of houses for sale and asked which home was hers. She pointed to it.

As the auction of her home progressed, the stranger bid on it. She had competition, but she kept raising her offer. Eventually, she won the bidding for the single mother's former home. Then she tracked the woman down.

"I came here to buy my son a house, but I realize now God sent me here to buy your house," she said. "I want to give it back to you."

This woman was heartbroken. She came to say good-bye to her home of many years, expecting to see it sold. But God had other plans. He made a way when it looked like there was no way. God remembered her.

✻ Today's Prayer to *It's Your Time* ✻

Father, help me see that the challenges I face are preparing me to better serve You.

✻ Today's Thought to *It's Your Time* ✻

When things aren't going my way, I have the opportunity to find out what I'm made of.

GOD KNOWS YOUR PURPOSE

DAILY READING 4:8

SCRIPTURE READING TO *IT'S YOUR TIME*   HEBREWS 10:19–39

So do not throw away this confident trust in the Lord.
Remember the great reward it brings you!
                                    HEBREWS 10:35 (NLT)

YEARS AGO, PAUL, A YOUNG Korean man, was dying from tuberculosis. One of his lungs had collapsed. As he lay in his bed at home, in so much pain, just waiting to die, he began to call out to his different gods one by one. He cried out to this god, "Please help me." There was no answer. He called out to another god. The same thing. And again, and again, and again.

Finally, in desperation, Paul said, "If there is any God up there anywhere, I don't ask you to heal me. I just ask you to show me how to die."

He was afraid to die. A few hours later, a young college student walking through the neighborhood felt what she called "an unexplainable love" drawing her to Paul's house. She went to his door not knowing why or what she was doing. A lady answered.

The college girl told her, "I know this sounds very, very odd, but is there anything I can pray with you about?"

The woman who answered the door was Paul's mother. She began to cry. "Yes, my son is on his deathbed," she said.

The college student went in. She prayed over Paul. That day, he gave his life to Christ. But Paul's life was not over. God supernaturally healed him. Today, many years later, Dr. Paul Yonggi Cho is pastor of the largest church in the world. He has more than five hundred thousand people in his church in South Korea.

God does not abandon His own. He knows the calling on your life. He knows what you were put here for. You need to do everything you can in the natural, but what you cannot do, God will supernaturally arrange.

I'm sure that young Dr. Paul felt alone and forgotten in all of his pain and suffering from tuberculosis. But he did not realize there was a Creator who knew him before he was born, a God who had granted him a purpose: to touch thousands. Sickness tried to stop him, but sickness is not too big for our God.

What is it that you think God cannot do? Do you have a family member, a relative who seems too far gone? Do you have a coworker, a friend, a neighbor who seems just too sarcastic, too cynical, too much of a partier?

I assure you: God has not written them off. God remembers them. And when God remembers, supernatural things can happen, and do! You, too, may be battling an illness and feel like you'll never get well. But we serve a God who is not limited to the natural.

You have an assignment. You have a destiny to fulfill. And no matter how bad it looks in the natural, no matter how many obstacles are in your path, God has not forgotten about you.

He will not take away His calling on your life.

You may be living far below where you're supposed to. You may be far away from where God wants you to be. But you might as well get ready, because the Most High God will not write you off. And when God remembers you, all the forces of darkness cannot keep you from fulfilling your purpose.

Sickness can't stop it. Your enemies can't stop it. Layoffs and foreclosures can't stop it.

God said He will lift you out of the pit, set your feet on a rock, and put a new song in your heart. "Unforgettable," anyone?

You need to get your fire back. Reclaim and fulfill your dreams. It may look like those dreams have died, but God can resurrect even dead dreams. Those promises may have been buried by disappointment, unfairness, sickness, or heartbreak, but God has not forgotten you. And when the Most High remembers, there is nothing that can keep you from your destiny.

✺ Today's Prayer to *It's Your Time* ✺

Thank You, Father, for breathing new life into my faith today.

✺ Today's Thought to *It's Your Time* ✺

God has not forgotten the destiny He created for me.

YOU ARE NOT FORGOTTEN

DAILY READING 4:9

SCRIPTURE READING TO *IT'S YOUR TIME*   I CHRONICLES 22

Now set your mind and heart to seek (inquire of and require as your vital necessity) the Lord your God. . . .
I CHRONICLES 22:19 (AMP)

Dr. WILLIAM H. "BILL" HINSON was the beloved pastor of Houston's First United Methodist Church for many years and a good friend of our family. He once told me that when his children were younger, he went out to pick up the newspaper one morning and saw a baby owl lying on the ground. His kids ran to look at it. They wanted to pick up the baby bird and hold it, but he stopped them. He called the local veterinarian, a friend.

The vet told him that sometimes strong winds blow baby owls out of the nest. Or sometimes the little owl gets overconfident and tries to fly before its wings are strong enough.

"In any case, it's good you didn't let the children pick it up," the vet said.

"Why is that?" said Dr. Hinson.

"Because if you go out and look up in the trees, there's a good chance you will see a mama owl looking down closely watching that baby owl," the vet said. "The mother will swoop down and attack if she thinks her baby is threatened, even when it is out of the nest and on the ground."

Dr. Hinson took his children back outside that day. They looked up and, sure enough, in the top of this pine tree there sat a large momma owl with these huge eyes staring directly down at them. She was standing guard over her fallen baby, ready to swoop in and protect it.

Dr. Hinson told his children something else the vet had said: "The mama owl would give her own life to protect her baby if she thought someone would harm it," he said.

Just like that mama owl, your Heavenly Father is looking down right now standing guard over you. Sometimes you may feel like the strong winds have knocked you down. At times you may feel like you're alone and forgotten. But if you can just remember to look up, you'll see those big heavenly eyes looking right back down at you. You'll see those eyes of love, those eyes of compassion, just waiting to come to the rescue, to protect, to defend.

Have faith that no matter where you are in life, no matter what comes against you, you are not alone. You are not forgotten. God remembers the dreams He's put on the inside. He remembers the promises you're holding on to. He remembers the sacrifices you've made.

You are unforgettable to our God. When He remembers you, supernatural things will happen. The dark clouds will give way to sunshine. The barren womb will conceive. The shaggy dog will warm you. The stranger will reach out and answer your prayers.

Who knows? One phone call may lead you to your dream. One conversation may deliver your promise. Know that you will see God show up and show out in amazing ways.

✸ Today's Prayer to *It's Your Time* ✸

Father, I choose to set my heart and mind on You today. I know that You have good things planned for me. Use me to be a blessing to others.

✸ Today's Thought to *It's Your Time* ✸

When I get up each morning, I will prepare myself for victory.

ADVERSITY CAN MAKE YOU STRONGER

———— ✨ ————

DAILY READING 4:10

SCRIPTURE READING TO *IT'S YOUR TIME*   ACTS 13:1–22

After removing Saul, he made David their king. He tes-
tified concerning him: 'I have found David son of Jesse
a man after my own heart; he will do everything I want
him to do.'

ACTS 13:22 (NIV)

THE MOVIE *THE PURSUIT OF HAPPYNESS* is about a friend of mine,
Chris Gardner, who is a smart, hardworking businessman hit by one
adversity after another. His business fails. He loses his savings. His wife
leaves him. He ends up homeless, raising his small son on the streets.
One day the father and son are shooting baskets with a new ball he'd
given the boy. As they are playing, the father says to his son, "I don't
want you to stay out here and play all day long because you'll probably
just be an average player. After all, that's all I was. You're usually just
as good as your dad. We have the same genes. So I don't want you to
waste a lot of time every day thinking that you'll ever really be good."

You could see his words taking the wind out of the boy's sails.
The son puts his ball down and he walks away feeling dejected. The
father sees the impact of his words and, feeling bad, he kneels, looks
his son in the eye, and says, "Listen here, son, don't you ever let anyone tell you that you can't be something great—not even me."

Often, those who will try to discourage you are simply imposing their own limitations upon you.

"That's as high as I went," they're saying. "You'll never go higher."

Don't believe it. Never allow anyone to convince you that your God-given dreams are out of reach. Not a family member, not a coach, not a so-called friend.

Listen to others. Be respectful. Welcome wisdom and support. But remember, when it's all said and done, the promise is in you. It's not in them.

Even King David had to rise above rejection. He had his doubters. His father and other family members did not see greatness in him. Yet David did not let the doubters determine his destiny. He said, "They may think I'm mediocre, but I know I have seeds of greatness. I know I'm equipped, I'm anointed, I will become everything God has created me to be."

The fact is that any time God is about to take you to a new level, you will face opposition. There will be new battles to fight, new obstacles to overcome, maybe people who doubt you, or speak poorly of you. I once heard somebody say, "New level, new devil."

It's easy to let negative voices discourage you. It's tempting to think, *Why is this happening? Why did they doubt me?* Or *Why did I get laid off?* Or *Why am I hit with one thing after another?*

But right beyond today's challenges are tomorrow's victories. New levels of success are just on the other side. Whenever God is about to take you to a higher level, you will face stronger opposition. There will be new battles to fight, new obstacles to overcome. The adversity can actually be the tool God uses to promote you. Many times our enemies will do more to catapult us to success than our friends will.

I know in my life there have been times when I was down. I didn't see a way out. It looked impossible. But I thought, *I cannot give up now. It would make my enemies too happy.*

Sometimes we can smile, not because we want to, not because we feel like it, but we smile because we will not give our enemies the pleasure of seeing us down. On the inside, you may be hurting. But on the outside, you should wear a smile on your face.

Do not let them see you defeated. Not out of pride. Not out of spite. But out of a quiet confidence, knowing that you are a child of the Most High God and He would not have allowed it if He did not have a purpose for it.

Deep down, know that you will come through challenging times promoted, increased, better off than you were before.

It's time to trust.

David would be known only as a shepherd boy if it were not for Goliath. The future king's greatest enemy was actually a tool used by God to promote him. David was called a man after God's own heart. God certainly loved David like He does each one of us. But what did God do? He sent him Goliath. The size of your problem reflects the promise of your future. If you have a big problem, don't get discouraged. That's a sure sign you've got a big future. Whenever God pits us against a Goliath, He always gives us the strength, the determination, the fortitude to overcome.

Even when the challenge is great and the bottom falls out, in the middle of that adversity there will be a supernatural strength, a peace that passes all understanding, a joy rising up in our spirit. God gives us exactly what we need.

Today's Prayer to *It's Your Time*

Father, thank You for giving me supernatural strength when faced with adversity.

Today's Thought to *It's Your Time*

The size of my problem reflects the promise of my future.

YOU AND GOD ARE A MAJORITY

DAILY READING 4:11

SCRIPTURE READING TO *IT'S YOUR TIME*   2 KINGS 7:3–11

> *So at twilight they set out for the camp of the Arameans.*
> *But when they came to the edge of the camp, no one was*
> *there! For the Lord had caused the Aramean army to*
> *hear the clatter of speeding chariots and the galloping of*
> *horses and the sounds of a great army approaching. . . .*
>   2 KINGS 7:5–6 (NLT)

I HAVE A FRIEND WHO started his company back in the early 1990s with only $150. He didn't have credit. He didn't have rich backers. All he had was a dream in his heart.

He tried to get a loan from his bank, but they turned him down. He went to twenty-six banks altogether; they all refused to loan him money. He had twenty-six good reasons to just give up and quit.

But when God puts a dream in your heart, when He puts a promise on the inside, it doesn't matter if you get rejected three *hundred* times. It doesn't matter what you don't have. It doesn't matter how big that giant is. Deep down, you know that you and God are a majority.

You are anointed to accomplish your dreams. You have been equipped by the Creator of the universe to overcome every obstacle. Forget what you lack. Look to who loves you. The same power who raised Christ from the dead lives inside you. You are well able.

My friend remembered this, and so he went to the twenty-seventh bank. There, his loan was approved. Today that young man runs a very successful company.

Like my friend and like David, you can defeat a giant with fewer resources. You can overcome an "untreatable" illness with God as your treatment. You can accomplish your dreams even though you lack the funds, the contacts, or the know-how.

You know that God's favor opens doors. You may have had twenty-six no's, but you believe that yes is waiting at number twenty-seven.

In the Old Testament, this huge army was about to attack a city. The soldiers were camped not far away, making plans for the attack. Four men crept out of the city toward the soldiers' camp. The men were lepers who figured they would probably be killed in the attack or die of their disease. And so instead of waiting for death, they made a move on the enemy's camp.

In the natural, it was an impossible situation. They seemed as good as dead. But these four men shared a faith that said, "Even though we're outnumbered a thousand to one, we will take a chance and see what our God will do."

The Scripture says that as the four closed in on the enemy's camp, God caused the sound of their footsteps to be multiplied. And to the enemy it sounded like a huge army was coming against them. The four men didn't realize what was happening. They didn't hear the magnified sound of their footsteps. They just kept on walking.

They feared they were about to be captured and killed. But when you dare to take steps of faith—even when your goal seems impossible, even when you've failed time after time, even when you don't have the education or connections—God will take what you have and multiply it.

You may not see God's hand at work. But behind the scenes, He is multiplying what you need. He is causing people to hear what He wants them to hear. He is lining up the funds you lack. He is making the connections you need.

Your enemy may be powerful but, as Goliath learned, all it takes is one smooth stone. Or like those four lepers, all you may need is the sound of your feet. God's amplified sound of four men marching shook the ground as if hundreds of thousands were descending. The soldiers outside the city ran away in fear. The four lepers did not understand what was frightening their enemy. They asked a fleeing soldier and he told them, "We're being attacked by a vast army. You've got to run for your lives."

Only then did it dawn on the lepers that *they* were the "vast army." They realized that when you stay in faith, God will cause people to see you the way He wants you to be seen.

You may feel weak. You may think you don't have what it takes. But here's the secret: Don't act on what you feel. Act on what you know.

In your mind you may feel afraid. But in your heart, know that you can do all things through Christ. If God be for you, who dare be against you?

∽ Today's Prayer to *It's Your Time* ∽

Father, thank You for causing people to see me the way You want me to be seen.

∽ Today's Thought to *It's Your Time* ∽

I should never doubt that I have exactly what I need because God will multiply what I have.

FOCUS ON FAITH

DAILY READING 4:12

SCRIPTURE READING TO *IT'S YOUR TIME*   1 SAMUEL 30:1–14

. . . David encouraged himself in the LORD his God.
1 SAMUEL 30:6 (KJV)

HELEN DREAMED OF BECOMING AN actress, but everyone told her she would never make it big because she was too small. She stood just five feet tall. So as a young woman she did stretching exercises and tried all sorts of ways to increase her height. None of them worked.

She didn't grow any taller, but instead of being discouraged and listening to the naysayers, Helen focused on being the best actress she could be. She took what God had given her and made the most of it.

Helen knew that others did not determine her destiny. She did not dwell on what the doubters said. Instead, she focused on what God told her deep inside. And Helen Hayes became one of the greatest actresses of her day and one of the few women to win a Tony, an Oscar, an Emmy, and a Grammy.

It is ironic that late in her career, she won some of her greatest critical acclaim for her movie role as Mary, Queen of Scotland— one of the tallest queens in history. When someone asked her how someone so short could possibly take on that role, Helen Hayes said, "I am an actress. I will act tall."

She understood that God gave her everything she needed. Like her, you should never allow other people to tell you what you don't have or what you can't do. Some don't believe that God can still heal. But it's too late to convince me. I've already seen how God healed my mother of terminal cancer in 1981. Some people don't think that your dreams can come to pass.

"Joel, you're just getting people's hopes up," they say. But it's too late to convince me. I'm living my dream. I've seen God do more than I could even ask or think.

When you defeat your Goliaths—your challenges and adversities—you establish yourself and you show others who you really are. Your victories prove God's anointing on your life. You will encounter naysayers, people who doubt you and say, "Ah, she's not that talented"; "He doesn't deserve that position"; or "Why did he marry her? She's not that attractive."

Know that you have more than talent. You have more than beauty. You have the favor of God. It's His anointing on your life.

I once heard somebody say, "Faith begins with stuffing your ears full of cotton." In other words, don't listen to the negative thoughts or comments. People will try to talk you out of your dreams. When I first started ministering I overheard people saying, "He can't preach. He's too young. He's not as good as his father."

So I found some cotton balls and put them in my ears. I've learned to always keep a fresh supply on hand. My father was the same way. When he started Lakewood in 1959 in a little run-down feed store, people told him, "Nobody will come to church out here. You're on the wrong side of town."

What did my dad do? Did he get down, discouraged, or give up?

Not my father. He put the cotton balls in his ears. He kept praying, kept believing, kept being his best. For forty years his church drew thousands of people every weekend. He built the foundation for everything Lakewood Church has become.

Many people let doubts take a stronghold in their minds. Something negative was spoken over them, they believed it, and suddenly it's holding them back. The first step to dealing with doubts is to determine how they were planted. Was it a family member who said you'd never be successful? Was it a teacher who predicted you'd never get an A? Was it a friend who said you'll never break your addiction?

Just because they didn't see it, just because they couldn't do it, doesn't mean you can't make it happen. Reprogram your thinking. Break free from the strongholds of doubt.

❧ Today's Prayer to *It's Your Time* ❧

Father, I know You would not have planted my dreams in my heart if You had not already given me the talent, the creativity, and the determination to see them come to pass.

❧ Today's Thought to *It's Your Time* ❧

People don't determine my destiny, God does.

WHEN YOU FACE ADVERSITY, YOUR DESTINY IS WITHIN REACH

DAILY READING 4:13

SCRIPTURE READING TO *IT'S YOUR TIME*   PSALM 3

> *Lord, how are they increased that trouble me!* . . .
> PSALM 3:1 (KJV)

WHEN HIS SON ABSALOM WAS trying to kill him and take over his kingdom, King David wrote the passage above. He was saying, "God, it looks like my enemies are multiplying." Sometimes we think, *I can make it if my neighbor is against me. I can dig in my heels and be strong if it's my coworker, or my boss, or my competitor.* But when it's our own family, when it's our own flesh and blood, it's easy to think, *God, this is just not right. I don't know if I can go on.*

David could have been overwhelmed. This could have been the point at which David faded off into the sunset, never to be heard from again. But the reason David was a champion—the reason he overcame every obstacle—can be found in this psalm's verse 3.

He didn't just stop with this one problem. He didn't just describe the situation and talk about how bad it was. He changed his focus. He said in effect, "God, I'm having all these problems. This is the worst thing I've ever faced." Here it comes, verse 3: "But You, O Lord, are a shield for me, my glory and the lifter of my head."

What is the message? Don't ever let the opposition have the final word. There are times when we say, "The doctor's report doesn't look good. I don't feel well. I don't really see how I will make it. But You, O Lord, I know You can make a way."

Always add the "but." "Yes, I'm having tough times, *but* I know God will see me through." "Yes, my retirement fund was cut in half, *but* I know He's Jehovah Jireh. He will supply all of my needs."

Or how about this? "Yes, I've had this addiction a long time, *but* I know it's only temporary. My chains are broken. Whom the Son sets free is free indeed."

Too often we leave out the "but." "Well, Joel, I've just been through so much. It's unfair."

"Yes, but God said He would pay you back double for that injustice."

"Yeah, but my problems are so big. Goliath is so large."

"Yes, but God said when the enemy comes in like a flood, He would raise up a barrier."

You may be in the middle of a struggle, but you've got to have the right perspective. That challenge was never meant to destroy you. It was meant to promote you. The very fact that you are facing adversity tells me that your destiny is within reach.

When David faced Goliath, deep down he knew something great was about to happen. He didn't get discouraged. He got encouraged by it. In the same way, I'll just declare it: When you come through that adversity, you will reach a new level. You will see God's favor like you've never seen it before. That problem will be the catalyst for God to open up supernatural doors.

I challenge you to be strong in the Lord. Put on the whole armor of God. Get up each day knowing not only who you are, but *whose* you are. No obstacle will hold you back.

❧ Today's Prayer to *It's Your Time* ❧

Father, thank You for helping me face challenges knowing that as long as I stay in faith and trust in You, I will not be defeated and, in fact, those challenges will promote me and leave me better off than before.

❧ Today's Thought to *It's Your Time* ❧

What was meant to harm me, God will turn to my advantage.

YOUR ANOINTING OF EASE

DAILY READING 4:14

SCRIPTURE READING TO *IT'S YOUR TIME*   PSALM 23

"You anoint my head with oil; my cup overflows."
PSALM 23:5 (NIV)

WE ALL GO THROUGH DIFFICULT times when we are not making much progress. We work hard but don't see promotion. We do our best in relationships, but they still seem stagnant. There are times in our finances when it is one struggle after another.

If we aren't careful, we can lose our enthusiasm and think this is the way it always will be. But Jesus said, "My yoke is easy and my burden is light."

There is something I call *the anointing of ease*. When you step into this anointing, what was difficult all of a sudden becomes easy. Things you struggled with are not a struggle anymore. There is a supernatural grace, a favor that lightens the load and takes off the pressure. Scripture describes this as God going before you and making crooked places straight, rough places smooth.

I was alone on a business trip, without the usual gang of Victoria, our kids, friends of kids, and nieces and nephews. I thought I was traveling light. But after my meetings, I ended up with a load of paperwork to carry in a big folder, along with my suitcase, a suit bag, and my briefcase with my computer.

I left my hotel room and headed down the hall to the elevator in a hurry to check out. But I was struggling to carry everything. I was concerned that I might be running late to catch my plane. I'd walked only about twenty steps down the hall when a young hotel bellman came out of nowhere.

"Sir, let me get that for you," he said.

He didn't grab just one bag. He took command of my entire load. Freed of my burdens, I walked with him toward the elevator where a crowd of other guests had gathered. It looked like everyone had decided to check out at the same time.

My bellman gave me a nod and whispered, "Follow me." He led me through a maze of hallways until we came to the service elevator. He punched a button and within seconds the doors opened to an empty elevator car. I was in the lobby and checked out within a few minutes, thanks to his help.

My ride to the airport went smoothly. I thought I was back on schedule, but then I ran into an unexpected delay. The security line at the airport was very long. It looked like it could take a half hour or more to get through. Again, I was fretting a bit when a gentleman wearing a badge walked up to me and said, "Follow me, Pastor Osteen."

I figured either I'd made the Terrorist Watch List or this was the favor of God blessing me again. Thankfully, it was God at work and not the FBI. The security man took my bags through for me. He commandeered a cart and drove me to my gate, telling me along the way that he recognized me from our television broadcasts and that he was glad to help me out.

My streak did not end there. I arrived home later that evening, relieved to be back with my family. After saying hello to everyone, I settled into my favorite chair. I was just planning to relax before dinner, but Victoria surprised me. She brought my meal to me on a tray. At that moment, I knew the day of miracles was not over!

You might think that God has more important things on His mind than helping someone check out of a hotel or catch a plane, that He has bigger things to deal with. But you should never forget *you* are God's biggest deal. You are the apple of His eye. You are His most prized possession.

Don't ever doubt that you are God's favorite child!

King David declared in Psalm 23:5 "You [God] anoint my head with oil . . ."

David was speaking of the type of oil that makes things flow. Whenever there is friction, whenever something is sticking, you apply oil to lubricate it and make it run more smoothly.

That's what God will do for you. He will anoint your head with oil. David next wrote of what happened after his anointing: "You anoint my head with oil; my cup overflows. Surely goodness and mercy will follow me all the days of my life."

I encourage you to stay in faith through hard times and when personal challenges linger. If you hold on to your faith, pray, and don't give in to depression or discouragement, better days will come. The first sign of this is when you experience an anointing of ease. When you step into an anointing of ease, you won't struggle anymore. You will feel a supernatural grace, a favor that lightens the load and takes off the pressure.

✎ Today's Prayer to *It's Your Time* ✎

Father in heaven, thank You for the anointing of ease. Today, I cast my cares on You knowing that You care for me. I ask for Your supernatural anointing to remove every burden and destroy every yoke of bondage in my life.

✎ Today's Thought to *It's Your Time* ✎

No matter how difficult things may seem, I will stand strong because His anointing of ease will carry me through!

EXPECT GOD'S ANOINTING

DAILY READING 4:15

Scripture Reading to *It's Your Time*   Matthew 11

For my yoke is easy to bear, and the burden I give you is light."

Matthew 11:30 (NLT)

Our daughter Alexandra was ten years old when she came up to me one day and asked for $10 to go to the movies. I told her to go to my bedroom closet and take a $10 bill from my wallet on the dresser.

"Thanks," she said.

But then she headed toward the front door instead.

"Aren't you going to get the money from my closet?" I asked.

Alexandra smiled. "I already did, Daddy. I knew you would say yes."

I was glad for her confidence in me. I love the fact that she knows I want to be good to her. God feels the same way about all of us. You may not realize it, but God has already said yes to His promises for you.

You don't have to beg God to be good to you. You don't have to beg God to help you. God wants to help you. The Scripture says that all of His promises are "Yes" and "Amen."

You need to go out every day knowing that God wants to help you. He wants to help you drive through traffic. He wants to help you shop for groceries, cook for your children, and deal with challenges at work.

Thank Him every day for that anointing of ease.

You need not worry. Your life will not be a constant struggle. Yes, there will be hard times and challenges, but don't you dare dwell on them. God has lined up the right breaks, the right opportunities, the right people in your future. Those hard times will end and give way to the best of times.

I love that God likes to outdo Himself. He didn't just meet our needs. He didn't just make our lives easier. He does more for us than we can think to ask of Him. With your anointing of ease, strangers will go out of their way to be kind to you. You will be blessed with creativity, wisdom, and good ideas.

When you are anointed with ease, you don't sweat the small stuff or the big stuff. You flow right through insults, frustrations, and challenges. God's anointing on your life will bring greater opportunities, helpful mentors, and important connections your way.

I encourage you to thank God for His anointing of ease. When you get in agreement with God by declaring His favor and His promises over your life, you won't drag through the day down and defeated. You won't receive the short end of the stick. The Scripture says, "Your cup will run over." Instead of feeling worn out, you'll run over with energy, good ideas, divine health, financial success, and joy.

✍ Today's Prayer to *It's Your Time* ✍

Father, thank You for Your favor in my life today. Thank You for causing me to be at the right place at the right time. Thank You for Your wisdom to make good decisions, Your grace to handle any challenge, Your strength to overcome any adversity, and Your faith to believe for big things.

❧ Today's Thought to *It's Your Time* ❧

If I expect God's anointing, I will run over with His blessings and favor.

GOD'S AMAZING GOODNESS

DAILY READING 4:16

SCRIPTURE READING TO *IT'S YOUR TIME*   EPHESIANS 2:1–10

For it is by grace you have been saved, through faith—
and this not from yourselves, it is the gift of God—
                                        EPHESIANS 2:8 (NIV)

SHERIAN CADORIA GREW UP "THE poorest of poor" in a small
Louisiana town in the 1940s and '50s. Her parents were tenant
workers on a cotton plantation. When she was three years old, her
father was injured in an accident and had to be hospitalized for the
rest of his life. The landlord of their farm kicked them out because
her father could no longer work.

Her mother loaded a wagon and moved into a two-room house
with no electricity or running water. She used pages from the Sears
catalog to cover all the holes in the walls, ceiling, and floor. As soon
as Sherian Cadoria could walk, she joined her mother, sister, and
brother in the cotton fields. By the time she was ten, she could pick
250 pounds of cotton a day.

Despite the poverty and the discrimination, Sherian learned that
she must make use of the gifts God had given her. Sherian's anointing of ease began when she enrolled in Southern University, a histor-
ically black college, in Baton Rouge. There, she entered a training
program for women planning on military careers. Even though the

Ku Klux Klan was demonstrating to stop black people from entering the military, she persevered. She was refused service in most restaurants and hotels, but she stayed in faith. She became the first woman to command an all-male battalion of military police.

This child of poverty who grew up picking cotton later served thirty-three months in Vietnam. She went on to a twenty-nine-year military career before retiring with the rank of brigadier general. She had become the highest-ranking woman in the military, the first African American female with the rank of general in the United States Army, and the first black woman to serve as a director on the Joint Chiefs of Staff.

If you'll stay in faith and be your best each day, God will amaze you with His goodness. You will look back and say, "Wow! God has been so good to me. I never dreamed I'd go so far, so fast."

⤜ Today's Prayer to *It's Your Time* ⤏

Father, thank You for seeing the best in me. I desire to become more like You each day.

⤜ Today's Thought to *It's Your Time* ⤏

God's approval is based solely on the fact that I am His child and He sees the best in me.

GOD DIRECTS OUR STEPS

DAILY READING 4:17

SCRIPTURE READING TO *IT'S YOUR TIME*   JOB 33:1–11

*The spirit of God hath made me, and the breath of the
Almighty hath given me life.*

JOB 33:4 (KJV)

I HAD TO DEAL WITH a difficult situation recently. It was a business matter. I needed some expert legal advice. I was on the road, so I called a lawyer friend of mine in Houston. He recommended one of his associates. Unfortunately, this expert had just left town on a two-week business trip.

I told my friend I didn't have two weeks to get this matter straightened out. I needed to get something set up before I returned home.

"Where are you?" he asked.

I told him.

"You've got to be kidding," my friend said. "That's exactly where my associate is headed. He'll be there in a few hours."

When I heard that, I knew God was still on the throne. There I was, thousands of miles from home, and God sent just the man I needed right to me. It turned out that he was staying five minutes away from me.

God directs every one of your steps. He lines up solutions to your problems. He lines up the breaks that you need. I want you to go out each day knowing that there is favor in your future. Restoration awaits. Healing and good breaks are in store for you.

Right now you may feel as though you are just trying to survive. I encourage you to keep pressing forward instead. God has another victory in your future. You don't know the anointing of ease awaiting you.

God will take you places you've never even dreamed of.

You will accomplish goals that you never thought possible. You will overcome obstacles that seemed insurmountable. You may get knocked down every once in a while, but you will never get knocked out. You are a child of the Most High God.

❧ Today's Prayer to *It's Your Time* ❧

Father, thank You for helping me accomplish what had seemed beyond my reach.

❧ Today's Thought to *It's Your Time* ❧

The most powerful force in the universe has me in the palm of His hand.

GOD IS BREATHING IN YOUR DIRECTION

DAILY READING 4:18

SCRIPTURE READING TO *IT'S YOUR TIME*   PSALM 126

> *. . . So those who went off with heavy hearts*
> *will come home laughing, with armloads of blessing.*
> PSALM 126:5 (THE MESSAGE)

FRIEDA, A SINGLE MOTHER WITH our church, was struggling to make ends meet. She was working long hours. She was hurting because she couldn't be with her children as much as they needed. She also had no free time for herself, no time to date or socialize.

This good hardworking woman told me she was feeling frustrated. Frieda couldn't see a way out of her situation. She didn't see any signs that her life would improve. Then, a few weeks later, the Creator of the universe provided an anointing of ease.

Frieda did not see it coming. She was about to give up. Fortunately, she stayed in faith and kept pressing forward. Others might have kept looking back, wondering why they couldn't catch a break. Frieda kept thanking God for His favor. And He directed her steps.

Shortly after we spoke, Frieda was approached by a neighbor she hardly knew. The neighbor had observed her struggles. He and his wife wanted to help. They bought her a new car. Grateful, Frieda then sold her old car, which enabled her to pay off some debt.

Now she doesn't have to work such long hours. That one unexpected gift relieved pressure.

"Joel, a load has been lifted off of me," she said.

God granted Frieda an anointing of ease to make her life better. You may face similar problems. You may be stressed about your future. I encourage you to find a place of peace. When you're in peace, you are in a position of power. You can say, "God, I trust You. I may not see a way, but I know You still have a way. So I will go out each day being my best, being productive at work, being a blessing to somebody else, and not looking back regretting the past. I'm pressing forward in faith."

When you do that you might as well get ready. You will receive God's anointing of ease. God knows every need you will ever have. You don't have to figure it all out: All you have to do is have faith. Dare to believe that God is in control.

Psalm 126 in the Message translation also says: "It seemed like a dream, too good to be true, when GOD returned Zion's exiles . . . And now, GOD, do it again— . . . So those who went off with heavy hearts will come out laughing with armloads of blessings."

That is God's dream. When you have a heavy heart, when life deals you a difficult blow, God wants to turn it around not only to bring you out but to bring you out with a smile, better off than you were before, "with armloads of blessing."

I don't know about you, but I've seen God do amazing things. I've experienced some firsthand. When I look back over my life, I can say with the psalmist, "It's like a dream too good to be true." Now my prayer for you is, "God, do it again. Do it for my friends. Show them Your unprecedented favor. Pour out Your goodness, Your blessings, Your mercy, Your grace. God, let their dreams suddenly come to pass."

Know this today: If God did it for me, He can certainly do it for you. Get up each day with expectancy. Have the attitude, "God,

I'm looking for my anointing of ease. I'm looking for armloads of blessings You have placed in my path."

Maybe you are struggling. But this is a new day. You are coming into your own. You will feel a supernatural strength. God will give you the grace to face your challenges.

You will get breaks you may feel are undeserved. Problems you've dealt with for years will suddenly disappear. You might as well get ready, because God will not simply bring you out. He will bring you out laughing, full of joy, full of faith, full of victory! It's time to trust.

⤜❧ Daily Prayer to *It's Your Time* ❧⤛

Father, thank You for my armloads of blessings.

⤜❧ Daily Thought to *It's Your Time* ❧⤛

When I release my faith, it will lead to the good things God has in store for me.

PART FIVE

IT'S TIME TO STRETCH

STEPPING INTO YOUR DIVINE DESTINY

─────── ✥ ───────

DAILY READING 5:1

SCRIPTURE READING TO *IT'S YOUR TIME*   HABAKKUK 2:1–8

> *For the revelation awaits an appointed time;*
> *it speaks of the end and will not prove false.*
> *Though it linger, wait for it;*
> *it will certainly come and will not delay.*
>   HABAKKUK 2:3 (NIV)

GABRIELA'S PHOTOGRAPHY BUSINESS WAS GOING great just a few years ago. She was shooting as many as fifty weddings a year in Houston. She finally needed a break to catch up with her husband and four kids.

Gabriela, who is known as "Gaby," took off a couple years. Unfortunately, when she was ready to return to her wedding photography business full-time, the economy was crashing.

Like millions of professionals and wage workers across the country, Gaby had to step back and look at other options during the recession. To her credit, she did not despair. Instead, Gaby decided to go after her dream.

"For ten years, I'd dreamed about being the photographer for my church, Lakewood Church," she said. "But I'd had that dream sitting up on a shelf collecting dust."

Gaby didn't tell me or Victoria about her dream of working for us. We were well aware of her photography talents because she had done weddings and family portraits for many of our church and staff members. She'd even made my brother, Paul, look good, and that's not easy to do!

We might never have known that she wanted to put her talents to work for us if her family had not encouraged her. Gaby woke up one morning, went into the bathroom, and found a message written on the mirror: *Who Are You?* Then, when she went to the kitchen there was another sign by the coffee pot: *Who Are You?* Another sign waited in the living room near her office: *Who Are You?*

Everywhere she looked, all over the house, her family had left the same sign urging her to pursue her divine destiny. Their faith and support got to Gaby. She finally made a move by asking for a five-minute meeting with one of our executives. When she completed her presentation, he welcomed her into the fold.

"The fact that you are in my office today is incredible," he said. "Just last week I had a meeting with Joel and we discussed the need to hire a photographer to cover all of what is going on here."

Today, Gaby is our church photographer, but only because she made a move and then God moved on her life. She is truly living her divine destiny. Every one of us has secret dreams and desires along with seeds of greatness implanted within us. You, too, have gifts to share with this world. There is buried treasure within you, waiting to be discovered. Your full potential has not been released yet. Your God-given divine destiny awaits you.

Too often, we procrastinate or we allow negative thoughts and self-doubt to discourage us from chasing our dreams. As a result our gifts go undeveloped. Sometimes we allow disappointments and failures to steal our confidence and, again, our treasures remain buried. Insecurities and low self-esteem can convince us that we have nothing special to offer.

God did not create you to be ordinary. He did not bestow gifts so that they could go undiscovered or grant potential that would be unfulfilled. Despite the discouragement you've heard, regardless of the hurts, challenges, or insults you've experienced, God gave you all that you need to achieve your destiny. All of the talents, skills, personality traits—all the treasures that lie within you—came from Him.

You have unique gifts and attributes. No one else has your exact combination. I urge you to understand that and to step into your destiny. The world will not be as bright as it could be if you don't release the full glow of your gifts and reflect God's glory.

No one can take your place. When God created you, He threw away the mold. Don't make the mistake of comparing yourself with someone else. If God wanted you to have their exact gifts, He would have given them to you. If He wanted you to look like them and share the same personality, He would have created you that way. To fulfill your destiny, you don't need what they have. You need only what lies within.

❧ Today's Prayer to *It's Your Time* ❧

Heavenly Father, thank You for the destiny that You have deposited into my heart. I choose to stand in faith knowing that You are working behind the scenes. Give me strength and wisdom to follow Your leading so that I can embrace all that You have for me.

❧ Today's Thought to *It's Your Time* ❧

God has planted seeds of greatness on the inside of me. He has predestined that those things in my heart come to pass.

THE MASTER WILL STEP
INTO YOUR LIFE

DAILY READING 5:2

SCRIPTURE READING TO *IT'S YOUR TIME*   EPHESIANS 2:1–10

*For we are God's masterpiece. He has created us anew
in Christ Jesus, so we can do the good things he planned
for us long ago.*

EPHESIANS 2:10 (NLT)

A FRIEND TOLD ME A story of a five-year-old boy who loved the
piano. At every opportunity, he would sit down and fiddle around
on the keyboard. He'd never had lessons or any kind of formal
training. The boy was often told that he was too small, too young
to play the piano. Despite those discouraging words, he continued
to practice and practice.

The only song he knew how to play was "Chopsticks." Just
a very simple tune. But he played it again and again. One day,
his father surprised him with tickets for the symphony. A world-
renowned Italian pianist was playing. This master musician was
one of the greatest piano players in modern times.

On the night of the concert, as they were walking to their seats
in the auditorium, the little boy saw the beautiful grand piano on
stage, behind the curtain. While no one noticed, he snuck over and

sat down on the piano bench. He then began to play his elementary version of "Chopsticks."

About that time, the curtain began to rise. Everyone expected to see the world-famous master pianist. Instead, they saw a little boy hunched over the piano playing "Chopsticks."

He was so caught up in his playing, the boy didn't realize anyone was watching. When he did notice, he was petrified. Just as he was about to get up and run off, the boy felt two big arms reaching around him. Then, two large hands landed on the piano keys next to his.

It was the master pianist. He whispered in the little boy's ear, "Keep playing." And as the little boy continued to play his simple rendition of "Chopsticks," the pianist joined in with a Beethoven symphony piece scored in the same cadence and the same key.

Under the direction of the master, the rest of the orchestra came in. First, he brought in the woodwinds, then the brass, then the percussion. The boy's father sat there with tears coming down his cheeks. He couldn't believe what he was hearing. He never dreamed the simple tune that he heard in his living room each day would no longer sound like "Chopsticks," but would become a full, beautifully orchestrated Beethoven symphony.

What was the difference? The master stepped in. Sometimes, you may feel like you don't have the talent, the wisdom, the know-how. The good news is, *God does.*

When you use what you have, the Master will step in. He will put His hands on top of your hands. He'll take what you think is very average—average gifts, average talent, average ability. But when the Master steps in, He'll put His *super* with your *natural* and *supernatural* things will begin to happen.

Like that little boy, you'll be amazed. You will think, *I know what I normally sound like. I know what I'm capable of. How did I end up like this?*

Here's how: The Master stepped in.

When I started ministering ten years ago, my first few sermons were so basic and so elementary. Like this little boy, I'm sure they sounded about like "Chopsticks."

I had never ministered before, but I was doing the best I could, using what God had given me. The negative thoughts bombarded my mind: *Joel, you don't have what it takes. You're not a minister. You're too shy. You're too quiet. You better stay in your safe zone.*

I had to keep shaking off those thoughts. I had to remind myself that I am a fully loaded person. I'm anointed. I'm equipped. I'm talented. I can do all things through Christ.

Then the Master stepped in. God put His hands on my hands. He put His voice in my voice. I discovered talents I didn't know I had. If you had told me ten years ago that one day I would minister in Yankee Stadium, I would have said, "Yeah, right. And you can land an airplane safely in the Hudson River."

My friend, when the Master steps in, supernatural things will happen. You may think you will never accomplish your dreams. You may think you don't have the talent, the resources, the connections. But know this: *God does.* You have to put a demand on your faith. If you play it safe all the time, you'll never know what's on the inside.

I believe that as you stretch your faith in the coming days, you will see the Master step in. You will have the courage to do things you wouldn't do before. You will discover an ability you didn't know was in you.

You will receive supernatural breaks. And just when you thought it couldn't get any better, God will bring in the brass—the right people.

Then the woodwinds—the right opportunity.

And before long, you will hear the sound of a beautiful orchestra. Your gifts and blessings will appear. You will know like I know: This is not just my talent. This is not just my ability. This is the Master joining in.

❧ Today's Prayer to *It's Your Time* ❧

Father, thank You for taking my "natural" and adding your "super" to it. I know You can do what man cannot do.

❧ Today's Thought to *It's Your Time* ❧

As I take steps toward my destiny, God will show up.

LET YOUR LIGHT SHINE

―――――――― ❧ ――――――――

DAILY READING 5:3

SCRIPTURE READING TO *IT'S YOUR TIME*   2 TIMOTHY 1

> *Wherefore I put thee in remembrance that thou stir up the gift of God, which is in thee by the putting on of my hands.*
>
> 2 TIMOTHY 1:6 (KJV)

A FRIEND TOLD US ABOUT her mother-in-law, who'd wanted to be an opera singer ever since she was a little girl. She was extremely talented. All through junior high and high school, she was chosen to sing the lead in class musicals.

But when it came time for college, her parents said, "You'll never make a living as an opera singer. That's not a good idea. You need to get a normal degree."

They talked her out of what she felt in her heart. She went on and earned her degree and lived a happy and a blessed life. Then, when she was ninety years old, she moved into a senior citizens' home. Her husband had gone to be with the Lord, and her mind was not as sharp as it should be. She suffered a little from dementia.

But every day in the seniors' home, she would stand in front of all the people and sing the most beautiful opera you could ever imagine. She sounded like an angel. In fact, people came from all over just to hear this ninety-year-old woman sing.

What was that? She had buried treasure on the inside. Her gift had been pushed down for nearly ninety years, but it was still alive just waiting to be released.

My challenge to you is this: Don't die with the music still in you. Share your talents and spiritual gift with this world. You can go farther than you think. You can accomplish more than you've accomplished.

⚒ Today's Prayer to *It's Your Time* ⚒

Father, thank You for helping me become what You created me to be.

⚒ Today's Thought to *It's Your Time* ⚒

I won't be surprised when I have wisdom beyond my years or accomplish things I'd thought were impossible because I know God is putting His hands on my hands.

PUT A DEMAND ON YOUR POTENTIAL

DAILY READING 5:4

SCRIPTURE READING TO *IT'S YOUR TIME*   ZECHARIAH 4

So he said to me, "This is the word of the LORD to Zerub-
babel: 'Not by might nor by power, but by my Spirit,'
says the LORD Almighty.

ZECHARIAH 4:6 (NIV)

WHEN I WAS GROWING UP, our next-door neighbors kept a big
German shepherd in their backyard. Even though their yard was
fenced off, they usually kept him on a leash. One day when I was
about eight or nine years old, I was in my backyard playing baseball with some friends and the ball went over into their yard. I
didn't think much about it. I'd been over there plenty of times.
Never had a problem.

So I climbed a small ladder over the six-foot fence. On the other
side, I picked up the ball. Then I saw their hundred-pound German
shepherd across the yard. He spotted me, too, and he came charg-
ing toward me at ninety miles per hour.

For some reason, he was not on the leash that day. When I realized that, my heart sank. I thought I was good as dead. I turned and
took off running toward the fence as fast as I could.

When I got there, all in one motion, I grabbed the top of the fence with one hand and I jumped as high as I could. Somehow I made it over that fence. I was just a little boy and I practically jumped over a six-foot fence.

After that, I never believed that "White men can't jump." I jumped that day. I promise you, I jumped!

That big ol' German shepherd helped me discover jumping potential I never knew I had. I had never jumped that high before. Fact is, I have never jumped that high since. But I'm glad to know at least it's in me.

That's what happens when you put a demand on your potential. It comes out. You'll be amazed at what you can do when you put yourselves in situations where you need to give something all you've got.

I heard recently about another situation like that. A guy was walking home late at night and decided to take a shortcut through the cemetery. It was dark, of course, and he stumbled and fell down into a great big hole dug earlier that day.

He tried and tried to get out, but it was too deep. He kicked and screamed and hollered and called for people but with no success. After about two hours he finally gave up. He sat down on the side to wait for morning.

Well, a few hours later an old drunk man came stumbling along and, sure enough, he fell into the same hole. He didn't see the man sitting over there already because he stayed quiet. The first guy watched as the drunken man screamed, hollered, kicked, and carried on just as he had when he first fell in.

The drunk tried to grab the side, kept falling back down, and again, with no success. Finally, the first guy decided to have some fun with the drunk.

"You'll never get out of here," he said in a deep, scary voice.

But you know what's interesting? He did!

Once again, you can do a *whole* lot more when you put serious demand on your potential! I want you to have a new boldness today, a new confidence. You are full of possibility. When I had to jump that fence to save my skin, I did it. The possibility was there, but I didn't know it until I was forced to find out.

If you develop that same sense of urgency, you will discover untapped potential, too. God is trying to plant new seeds in your heart today. You've got to enlarge your vision. Believe that you do have what it takes. I pray every day, "God, stretch me. Give me new opportunities. Help me to grow." When they come I do my best to take that step of faith.

It's easy to get comfortable. It's easy to settle where we are and just think, *Hey, I'm doing as well as anybody I know.*

But you're not competing against them. You are trying to be the best you can be. You know when you're stretching. You know when you're pushing yourself.

Don't wait for the dog to come chasing you before you try to jump higher than ever before. Stir up your gifts on the inside. God is saying, "I will take you somewhere that you've never been before. I will open new opportunities. I will give you new ways to increase. Are you prepared?"

You can overcome every obstacle. You can fulfill every dream. You are anointed. You are equipped. You are empowered. This is your season to reach new heights. I believe God is about to release the hidden treasure buried in you. He will grant you new opportunities to draw out your potential.

✺ Today's Prayer to *It's Your Time* ✺

Father, thank You for breathing favor in my direction.

✺ Today's Thought to *It's Your Time* ✺

When I take a step of faith and do what God has put in my heart He will breathe favor upon me.

KEEP THE FIRES BURNING

DAILY READING 5:5

SCRIPTURE READING TO *IT'S YOUR TIME*   1 SAMUEL 30

> *And David was greatly distressed; for the people spake*
> *of stoning him, because the soul of all the people was*
> *grieved, every man for his sons and for his daughters: but*
> *David encouraged himself in the LORD his God.*
>
> 1 SAMUEL 30:6 (KJV)

ONE NIGHT, I WAS WATCHING a great National Football League playoff game. The score was going back and forth. In the second half, the field goal kicker for the New York Giants twice had an opportunity to win the game. The distance was within his range. But both times he missed. It's a big deal to miss once in professional football, but in a playoff game to miss twice in one half is really something else. His coach was beside himself.

Then the game went into overtime. The Giants got the ball back. They were marching down the field, trying to score a touchdown. The first team to score wins in overtime, but once again the Giants were stopped before they could score a touchdown.

It was fourth down and the coach had to make a decision. Would he allow his kicker to try another field goal? This one would be farther than the two he had already missed. Or would the coach play it safe and punt the ball away?

The cameras showed the coach on the sideline deliberating what to do. He had only about twenty or thirty seconds to make a decision. He looked up and down the sideline to see what the kicker thought. He couldn't find him anywhere.

Finally, he looked on the field. The kicker was already lined up in position ready to kick the field goal. When the coach saw his kicker's confidence and determination, he gave him the go-ahead to attempt the field goal. This time, even though it was farther, the kicker put it straight through the uprights and won the game for the Giants!

You may have fallen short of your goal a couple of times in life, maybe a couple hundred times. We all have. But my question to you is, *Are you running back on the field?*

Do you still know, like the Giants kicker, that you've got it on the inside? Don't let your mistakes, your disappointments, life's failures keep you from pressing forward. The potential is still in you. You're well able to do what God's called you to do.

My prayer for you is that before you leave this earth, all of your potential will be released. Not one dream, not one gift, not one promise, not one God-given desire will go left unfulfilled.

You don't realize it, but you can't die yet. You had too much left in you. You have too much potential. God will not allow your gifts to be wasted. You might as well put up that rocking chair. It's not time to retire, it's time to refire.

Get ready. God will give you new opportunities and more time to share your gifts with the world. I read about a ninety-three-year-old woman who just graduated from college. If she can do it at ninety-three, you and I can do it at twenty, at forty, at sixty, at eighty.

Get your fire back. The moment you quit planning for your future is the moment you quit living. The day you quit being excited about what God has in store is the day you go from living to just breathing. You need to have the right attitude, the right vision for your life.

❧ Today's Prayer to *It's Your Time* ❧

Father, thank You for giving me the determination to live up to Your expectations.

❧ Today's Thought to *It's Your Time* ❧

I am a fully loaded person, totally equipped.

STAY OPEN FOR SOMETHING NEW

DAILY READING 5:6

SCRIPTURE READING TO *IT'S YOUR TIME*   JOSHUA 1:1–9

*Have not I commanded thee? Be strong and of good
courage; be not afraid, neither be thou dismayed: for the
Lord thy God is with thee whithersoever thou goest.*

JOSHUA 1:9 (KJV)

MARY LEE BENDOLPH GREW UP picking cotton. She lived in one
of the poorest parts of the country. She and her neighbors often
struggled to survive. Yet even in the worst of times, Mary Lee and
her friends made quilts. They stitched together patches from old
pants, shirts, sheets, and towels to keep their loved ones warm.

While they stitched, the quilters sang gospel songs, read the Bible,
and prayed for God's blessings. The quilts were a big part of life in
their little Alabama town. So Mary Lee and the other quilters were
understandably wary when an art collector showed up one day asking about them. He praised their quilts and offered to buy them.

Some of the quilters refused, even though the collector offered
hundreds of dollars. Mary Lee was among those who decided to
trust him. You see, she was open for something new.

"I always prayed for the Lord to make a better way for me and
He did," she said later.

The art collector bought Mary Lee's quilts and others from

the women of Gee's Bend, Alabama. He exhibited and sold them around the world. To the amazement of the quilters, their creations were praised as "works of genius." One New York art critic called their quilts "the most miraculous works of modern art America has produced."

Today, quilts from Gee's Bend sell for thousands and thousands of dollars each. Mary Lee and her fellow quilters are regarded as great artists. Their experiences show that successful people know how to change with the times. They don't get stuck in a rut doing the same thing, the same way year after year. They're constantly evaluating where they are and what they're doing. They make adjustments so they can improve.

Just because something worked five years ago doesn't mean it will work today. We have to stay open to change. We can't get so set in our ways that we won't try anything new. This is why many people lack enthusiasm. There's no freshness in their lives. Every time an opportunity comes for change, for promotion, for increase, because they're not used to it, they shrink back. They don't realize that is keeping them from climbing to the next level.

In the coming days don't be surprised if God brings new opportunities across your path. You may be offered a position that you feel is over your head. You may have an opportunity to change careers or to go into a different field. Or, if you are single, God may bring somebody new into your life, a divine connection.

You will be tempted at first to play it safe and think about all the reasons why you can't make a change. Maybe you've been hurt in the past. You can't get into that new relationship. You are not qualified for that new position. You may be afraid of failing. But if you are to experience God's best, you must be willing to take a risk. You can't get stuck thinking that it can only happen one way. God likes to do new things.

God has new victories out in front of you. You may have been through some disappointments in the past, but now it's time to arise and shine and believe again, dream again, and hope again. We have to be open for the new tasks set before us by God, and believe by faith that He will give us the strength, wisdom, and willpower to achieve what looks impossible. We should not get stagnant, thinking "This is all I know how to do," nor should we live in the past.

When the Old Testament prophet Moses died, Joshua was left to lead the Israelites across the Jordan River. He remembered how Moses, in the past, held up his rod and parted the Red Sea. But in Joshua's new circumstance, God had a different plan. He had to stay open for the new direction; once he did, and obeyed, despite how things were done in the past, how "things once were," God lead him in new leadership and the waters parted, and the people were able to go through on dry ground. We need to be like Joshua and adopt the attitude "If it didn't work one way, I'm not going to get defeated and give up. I know God has another way."

✖ Today's Prayer to *It's Your Time* ✖

Father, thank You for loving me. I cast all of my cares on You and set my heart on You today.

✖ Today's Thought to *It's Your Time* ✖

If I remember to put on a positive new attitude and stay open to new opportunities, God will continually lead me and bring me to a place of blessing.

BE OPEN FOR NEW OPPORTUNITIES

DAILY READING 5:7

SCRIPTURE READING TO *IT'S YOUR TIME*   1 PETER 5

*So humble yourselves under the mighty power of God,
and at the right time he will lift you up in honor.*

1 PETER 5:6 (NLT)

UNTIL WORLD WAR II, SWISS watch manufacturers controlled 90 percent of the global market. They were very good at what they did. They made beautiful, precise watches. No one could compete with them. But in the late 1960s, researchers in Switzerland presented the major manufacturers with a new concept—the electronic quartz watch. This watch did not have to be wound. It had a battery. It was much more precise than most mechanical watches and required less maintenance.

The major Swiss watchmakers did not welcome the innovation. Bound by tradition, the watchmakers, of all people, did not accept that times change. The creators of the quartz watch were not discouraged. They took their innovations to the International Watch Fair. There, two Asian manufacturers from outside the watch industry saw the potential of the new quartz design. They jumped on the quartz concept and moved quickly to corner the market. Soon they were selling more watches than any other manufacturers in the world.

The Swiss watchmakers were down but not out. They learned their lesson. They went for a change. They formed a national conglomerate. Then they came up with inexpensive, colorful Swatch watches that helped them get back in the game.

We have to stay open to new ideas. When something new comes across your path, don't be closed-minded. Don't just rule it out and say, "That's not for me." Be open for new opportunities.

We are not supposed to live off of past victories. Some people are always talking about "the good old days." That's fine; I've had a lot of good old days. I hope you have, too. But can I tell you something? God has some good *new* days for you, too.

Your greatest victories are not behind you. They are still out in front of you.

I want to light a new fire on the inside of you. You may have lost your passion. You may have gone through disappointments. Things might not have worked out—and now you're in that rut, just doing the same thing, the same way. But this is a new day. God is getting you prepared for new things He's about to do. When those opportunities come across your path, don't you dare think, *I can't do this. I don't have those skills. This is not what I'm used to. I'm too old.*

No, shake off all of that and say, "I am well able. I am equipped. I am anointed. I am empowered. I'm going to step into a new level of my destiny."

Today's Prayer to *It's Your Time*

Father, I thank You for turning things around for my good and Your glory.

Today's Thought to *It's Your Time*

I need to always remember that God gives me challenges to make me stronger.

STIR UP WHAT GOD HAS PUT ON THE INSIDE

DAILY READING 5:8

Scripture Reading to *It's Your Time*   Joshua 4

> *The priests who were carrying the Ark stood in the middle of the river until all of the Lord's commands that Moses had given to Joshua were carried out. Meanwhile, the people hurried across the riverbed. And when everyone was safely on the other side, the priests crossed over with the Ark of the Lord as the people watched.*
>
> Joshua 4:10–11 (NLT)

Today we take iPhones, iTunes, and iPods for granted because they are so common. We forget that, like the Bible's Job, Steve Jobs had his setbacks and challenges. He started his first business in his parents' garage at the age of twenty. Within ten years, Apple was a $2 billion company. But then, his own board of directors fired Jobs from his own business!

Did he become a victim? No. He said that getting fired from Apple was the greatest thing that ever happened to him! Today, it would be hard to disagree with that. After Jobs built up two more successful companies and sold them for billions, Apple realized its mistake. They brought Jobs back. He restored Apple as one of the most successful and innovative companies in the world by introducing an entirely new line of products and creating lucrative new markets.

Sometimes challenges force us to try new approaches that bring greater rewards than we'd dreamed of achieving. Be willing to stretch yourself. Stir up what God has put on the inside. If you don't have a dream, you're not really living. You're only existing. You have to have a reason to get out of bed each morning, something that motivates you, something that you're passionate about. Maybe at one time you had a dream, but you went through some disappointments. But here's a key: When one dream dies, dream another dream. Just because it didn't work out the way you had it planned doesn't mean God doesn't have another plan.

You cannot allow one disappointment or even a series of disappointments to convince you that your dream never will happen. Thomas Edison was described as "unteachable" early in his schooling. Later, as a scientist and inventor, he had one failure after another in his efforts to develop an incandescent electric lightbulb.

Still, Edison did not despair. He kept dreaming another dream.

"I have not failed," he said. "I have just found ten thousand ways that won't work."

We all know that Edison eventually turned on the lights. You will, too, if you stay in faith and stay open to change.

You may have tried and failed, but understand this: A failure is not a denial; it's just a delay.

Negative thoughts will come: *It's over. You're too old. You blew it. You had your chance.* These thoughts will try to convince us to give up on what God has placed in our hearts. But you must dig in your heels and say, "Thanks, but no thanks. It may not have worked out my way, but I know God has another way. I will not sit around and live my life defeated. I will rise up and dream a new dream."

This is what Joshua had to do. He stayed open to things happening a different way. After Moses died, Joshua was chosen to lead the people of Israel. They were headed toward the Promised Land. They came to the Jordan River. They needed to get across, but there was no bridge.

Joshua remembered that his predecessor, Moses, had held up his rod and parted the Red Sea. I'm sure he thought God would tell him to do it the same way. I can even imagine Joshua climbs to the top of the hill, holds up his rod, and says, "God, please part this river." He's praying. He's hoping. He's believing.

This is the first real test of his leadership. Everyone is watching closely, thinking, *Let's see if he has what Moses had. Let's see what Joshua is made of.*

He holds up the rod. But wouldn't you know it? Nothing happened. The waters didn't budge. He easily could have thought, *I must not be the right one. It worked for Moses, but it didn't work for me.*

No. Joshua understood this principle. He stayed open for something new. God told him to tell the priests to start marching toward the waters. And the moment their feet touched the waters, the river would part.

The priests walked to the water. The closer they came, the more people tried to talk them out of it. "You'd better not keep going. You better not listen to Joshua. You will surely drown."

It didn't faze them. They just kept walking, doing as God said. And sure enough, as soon as their feet touched the water, it began to pull back. People were able to go through on dry ground, just like they'd done with Moses.

What am I saying? God chose to do it a different way with Joshua than He did with Moses. Had Joshua been set in his ways and closed-minded, he would have missed out on God's best. But Joshua's attitude was: *If it didn't work one way, I will not be defeated and give up. I know God has another way. So I will keep trying. I will keep believing. I will keep pressing forward until I find that right way.*

✑ Today's Prayer to *It's Your Time* ✑

Father, thank You for showing me Your way to Your best life for me.

✑ Today's Thought to *It's Your Time* ✑

I may have to face some closed doors before I come to those that open for me.

BE WILLING TO DREAM A NEW DREAM

DAILY READING 5:9

SCRIPTURE READING TO *IT'S YOUR TIME*   ISAIAH 60:1–7

Arise, shine; for your light has come,
And the glory of the LORD has risen upon you.
ISAIAH 60:1 (NAS)

MARY MCLEOD BETHUNE WAS THE youngest of seventeen children. She was born in South Carolina back in the late 1800s to slaves. In spite of all the odds, she got a good education and even went to college. From the time she was a little girl she had a desire to go to Africa one day and teach children. She had this dream year after year. She just knew that one day she would be teaching those students.

As she neared graduation from college, she sent her application to a well-known missionary organization. She was a straight-A student with an impeccable reputation. You couldn't meet a finer young woman. Week after week, she was waiting, hoping, praying, believing that she would get accepted. But one day came the news she didn't want to hear. For some reason she had been turned down. She was devastated. She said it felt as if something died inside her that day.

Working with children in Africa was what Mary Bethune wanted to do with her life. But remember, when one door closes, if you will stay in faith, God will open up another door. Instead of sitting around thinking about how bad life had treated her and what didn't work out, she put on a new attitude.

"If I can't teach the students over there, then I'll teach the students here," she said. Mary Bethune decided to open her own school. She didn't have any money, had no building, no equipment, but where there's a will, there's a way. She found cardboard boxes and used them as desks. She strained red berries so her students could use the juice as ink in their pens. She and her students raised money for their books every week by hauling thousands of pounds of garbage down to the local dump.

Several years went by. A college nearby noticed what was going on and asked Mary's school to join forces. The two schools became Bethune-Cookman College, which is now known as Bethune-Cookman University in Daytona Beach, Florida. Mary Bethune went on to become the first African American woman to be a college president. In 1932, President Franklin Roosevelt appointed her as an advisor to his cabinet, making her the first African American woman to serve as a presidential advisor.

If things don't work out the way you had hoped, don't sit around all defeated. Dream a new dream. God is still in control. He would not have allowed the door to close unless He had something better in store. Life may not be fair, but know this: God is fair. Nothing you've been through has to keep you from your destiny. If you didn't get the job you wanted, apply for another job. If you can't teach the students overseas, teach the students here. Put on a new attitude. God has you in the palm of His hand. He has already planned out your days for good. He holds victory in your future.

Ask yourself if you are really living today. Or are you just existing? You must stir up the dreams that have been pressed down. The Scripture says in Isaiah 60:1, "Arise, shine; for your light has come . . ." It doesn't say that your light "will come." It says your light "has come." If you knew the great things God had in your future, you wouldn't go around discouraged and negative. You would go out each day with a smile on your face and a spring in your step.

As a young man, my father sold popcorn in the Isis Theatre in Fort Worth, Texas. He was raised in extreme poverty. At the age of seventeen my father gave his life to the Lord. God called him to preach. He ministered in the prisons, the rest homes, on the streets, anywhere he could find. My dad was married at an early age. But unfortunately that marriage didn't work out. His dreams were shattered. He left the ministry and didn't think that he would ever preach again.

For several years he went into the insurance business. He was very good. He excelled at what he did. But down deep inside he knew the call of God was still on his life. He didn't feel worthy. He didn't feel like he deserved it. Everyone around him was telling him, "You're washed up. You'll never be in ministry again. You'll never have a family." It's funny. Sometimes when we're down, people try to keep us down. But this is what I love about God: He lifts the fallen. He gives hope to the hopeless. His mercy is bigger than any mistake we could ever make.

I don't believe that divorce is God's best. But unfortunately sometimes it happens. I'm not for divorce, but I am for divorced people. Your life does not have to stop just because a relationship came to an end. God still has a plan. Arise and shine. That means get up from that discouragement. Shake off that self-pity. Receive mercy for your mistakes.

Arise—that's the first thing. And then number two, you must shine. Put a smile on your face. Get your enthusiasm back. Laugh again. Enjoy your life. Take up new hobbies. Find some new friends. Buy some new clothes. It's not enough to just arise. Shine! That is an act of your faith. When you shine, you're announcing not only to yourself, not only to your friends, but you're saying to the enemy, "I will not live my life in regrets. I will not beat myself up over the mistakes I've made. I know God has another plan, so I will arise and shine."

My father had all these thoughts telling him, *You'll never be in ministry. You'll never have a family again.* But God is a God of restoration. He will take what was meant for your harm and use it to your advantage. Several years later my father left the insurance business and returned to the ministry. Things began to flourish. One day he met my mother. They fell in love and married. God blessed them with five children.

I often think that we wouldn't be here today if my father had not stayed open to a plan different than his. Had he not been willing to dream a new dream, he never would have met my mother. I probably never would have been born. There may not have been a Lakewood Church.

In life there will always be voices telling us, "You blew it. You had your chance. It's over. Just settle where you are." Don't believe those lies. If you get knocked down, get back up again. It's not over until God says it's over. My father went from being a popcorn salesman, to a minister, to an insurance salesman, back to being a minister. That tells me God knows how to connect the dots.

≈ Today's Prayer to *It's Your Time* ≈

Father, thank You for planting great things in my future.

≈ Today's Thought to *It's Your Time* ≈

I would not be alive if God didn't have something great in my future.

GOD WILL DELIVER YOU
TO YOUR FINAL DESTINATION

※

DAILY READING 5:10

SCRIPTURE READING TO *IT'S YOUR TIME*　　　　PSALM 30:1–12

> . . . *Weeping may last through the night,*
> *but joy comes in the morning.*
> 　　　　　　PSALM 30:5 (NLT)

IN THE EARLY 1900S, FARMERS across the South were facing a major challenge. A tiny little insect called the boll weevil had migrated from South America and was quickly destroying their crops. They tried everything they could do to get rid of it. They exterminated with all kinds of pesticides. They even came up with new formulas they had never used before, still to no avail. Eventually, all they could do is sit back and watch their crops and their livelihood be eaten away. They were so discouraged. It looked like it was over.

But then, as farmers were feeling defeated and down, scientist George Washington Carver came up with an idea. He said, "Instead of planting our normal cotton crops that we know won't survive, why don't we try something new. Let's plant peanuts."

They looked at him like a cow at a new gate.

"Peanuts?" they said. "We could never make a living off of peanuts."

But Carver, a botanist, eventually talked them into it. He explained that peanut oil was used in hundreds of products: everything from cosmetics to paints, plastics to nitroglycerin.

Better yet, he had discovered that boll weevils did not like the taste of peanuts. The first peanut crops took off and flourished like nothing they had ever seen before. The farmers made more money in several months than they normally made in a whole year. In fact, even when the boll weevils left, the farmers didn't go back to their cotton crops. They stuck with peanuts, producing more than any country in the world.

God has a plan. You may have some boll weevils bothering you right now, but don't worry. There are some peanuts in your future. What you may think is a set*back* is really a set*up* for a greater *comeback*.

I love the fact that the boll weevils did not like the taste of peanuts. That tells me God always has something in my future that the enemy cannot touch. He always has some way to prosper me, some way to heal us, some way to restore us, some way to bring our dreams to pass.

Even when it looks difficult, even when things don't work out, just remind yourself, "These boll weevils may be causing me some problems. They may not even go away. But really, I'm not worried about it. I know they can't touch my harvest. God has given them a distaste for what belongs to me."

So think of this: That person at the office who always gets on your nerves and annoys you; next time you see him, just think to yourself, *He's just a boll weevil. He can't touch my harvest!*

This shows us how God's plan is better than our plan. Had it not been for the boll weevils, the farmers never would have tried peanuts. They would have just kept producing their usual crops over and over, all the while missing out on the abundance that should have been theirs.

When you face an adversity, that setback, that disappointment, you don't know where it's taking you. You've heard the saying, "When you're down to nothing, God is up to something." When it looks like your crops are being eaten up, God is not on the throne saying, "Oh, man. What will I do? Who let the boll weevils out?"

No, God is in complete control. He has a way even when we don't see a way. Here's the key: Had those farmers not been open for something new and been willing to reinvent themselves, they could still be sitting around saying, "Just my luck. Too bad for me. A little insect ruined my future."

Nothing has to destroy your future. When one dream dies, dream another dream. Try something else. If you hold up your rod and the rivers don't part, walk to the waters. God has another plan. Be willing to get out of your comfort zone. Keep a freshness in your life. Don't be satisfied living off past victories. God has new victories out in front of you.

You may have been through some disappointments, but it's time to arise and shine. It's time to dream a new dream. It's time to believe again. If you'll put on this new attitude and stay open to new opportunities, God will lead you to the peanuts when the boll weevils show up.

You may have been through a disappointment or something that didn't work out. Maybe it was even your fault. But God is saying, "I still have a plan. Dream a new dream." Get your fire back. Get your enthusiasm back. Just because it didn't happen one way doesn't mean it's over. When life deals you a lemon, God can make lemonade. He can take your mess and turn it into your message. It's time to arise and shine.

✑ Today's Prayer to *It's Your Time* ✑

Father, thank You for bringing my dreams to pass.

✑ Today's Thought to *It's Your Time* ✑

When it looks like my darkest hour, God will turn it around, restore me, and bring me out of the darkness to my brightest days!

FIND YOUR PLACE OF BLESSING

DAILY READING 5:11

Scripture Reading to *It's Your Time*   I Kings 17

> *Then the word of the LORD came to Elijah: "Leave here, turn eastward and hide in the Kerith Ravine, east of the Jordan. You will drink from the brook, and I have ordered the ravens to feed you there."*
>
> I Kings 17:2–4 (NIV)

My friend Reuben is a mechanic with his own auto repair business. For years his shop was on a little side street in an out-of-the-way industrial area. He built up a loyal clientele, but it was a struggle. Some weeks he could barely pay the bills.

Then one day, Reuben was driving on the freeway in Houston when he saw a "For Lease" sign on a big building only a block off that major road. Something clicked. He copied the phone number on the sign and called it that afternoon. The commercial real estate agent told him the building was still available.

Reuben went back with the real estate agent and inspected the vacant building, inside and out. Then he went home and prayed for God's guidance. Afterward, he felt a sense of peace, as if buying that building was part of God's plan.

So Reuben made the move to the new location. It was less than a mile from his old place, but the next year, his business increased ten times over!

What made the difference? Reuben moved to his place of blessing.

Could you be in the wrong place at the right time? Could it be that, like Reuben, you are just a little short from where you need to be to become all you can become?

I'm not talking just about locations for business or living. Maybe you are situated in the wrong relationship, or maybe you are in the right state of the country, but the wrong state of mind due to stress or anger. Maybe you need to hang up a hangout that is not your true place of blessing?

If you are not growing, if you feel unfulfilled, unsettled, and out of place, it could be that you need to move on to a better place. There is a place God has designed where opportunities find you, a place where His blessings overtake you.

God created the oceans, and then He created fish and other marine life to swim in His waters. He created land, and then He populated the planet with man and animals.

Location, location, location is not just a Realtor's slogan. God has always been careful about matching his creatures to the places where they will flourish. He didn't put polar bears in the Mojave Desert. He didn't place sharks and rays in the Rocky Mountains.

In the same way, God has a particular place for each one of us, a place where each of us will find our highest purpose, where we will thrive and reflect God's greatness. He has a specific job for you, in a specific community, where you are surrounded by specific people positioned to help you find fulfillment.

Your location is extremely important. God will not bless you just anywhere. He will bless you when you are where you're supposed to be physically, emotionally, mentally, and spiritually. I encourage you to find that place. Don't settle for anything less than the best God has to give you.

You can tell your place of blessing by how it feels to you. Your senses and your spirit will tell you, *This is where I am supposed to be*. It's like the game Victoria and I played with our children when they were younger. We would hide favorite toys, books, or candy around the house and ask Alexandra and Jonathan to find them. When they moved in the direction of the "hidden treasure," we would tell them they were getting warmer and warmer until they'd be right there and we'd say, "You're red hot!" If they went in the wrong direction, away from the hidden goodies, we'd say, "You're getting colder. Now you're freezing cold!"

I would encourage you to always move toward the places that warm your spirit, and move away from those that leave you cold. Move to the place that feels right to you and await God's blessing there.

Today's Prayer to *It's Your Time*

Father, thank You for leading me and directing my steps.

Today's Thought to *It's Your Time*

The Bible says when my heart is in the place of blessing, the rest of my life will be in the place of blessing, too!

YOU MIGHT HAVE TO MAKE A MOVE

DAILY READING 5:12

SCRIPTURE READING TO *IT'S YOUR TIME*   EXODUS 14:15–21

> *Then the LORD said to Moses, "Why are you crying out*
> *to me? Tell the people to get moving!*
>   EXODUS 14:15 (NLT)

In the Old Testament, the children of Israel followed the cloud by day and the pillar of fire by night. Sometimes the cloud remained at the same location for two or three months. They camped there until signs changed. Sometimes, the cloud would move every day for a week. So when they rose each morning, the first thing they had to do was to check the cloud.

I'm sure there were times that they wanted to move because they didn't like the location or they were surrounded by enemies. But the cloud stayed, so they stayed. At other times, I can imagine they'd awaken to see the cloud moving and think, *We just set up camp. We like this place. We're comfortable. Let's stay here.*

Yet they understood their blessing was connected to being at the right place. They knew they wouldn't have the food, the supplies, the protection they needed unless they followed the cloud. They had to do their part and reach their place of blessing so they could enjoy God's favor.

If you miss the signs, whether clouds or pillars of fire, or just a nagging feeling deep inside, you could become trapped in a bad place. Negative environments will keep you from going and growing. Some are infested with temptations, distractions, or bad attitudes. Do you need to move onward and upward? Life is too short to waste time in the wrong place, blocked from God's full blessing.

Some longtime friends of ours were still in their twenties when they followed God's guidance and moved to Montgomery, Alabama. With no experience in broadcasting, this young faith-filled couple worked to build the state's first full-power Christian television station.

It was no easy task. With little money, they had to scavenge for old equipment tossed out on the curb by other television stations. Often they worked without air-conditioning and did repairs and painting themselves to save money. Still, over five years they built up a successful television ministry. They were happy and fulfilled in their work.

Then about six years later, they saw the signs from God calling them to a new location and a greater blessing. They were called to sell their Montgomery station and move to a bigger market. It didn't seem to make sense to leave an established station with nothing lined up. They had no station, no contacts, no financing waiting for them in the bigger city. All they had was their faith. They stepped out not knowing what lay ahead.

Then, out of the blue things began to fall into place. Through a series of unusual events, they ended up with an independent station. Within seven years they had not just one station but an entire network.

Our friends followed the signs and reaped the rewards. Their place of blessing moved. Had they not been sensitive, had they been stuck in a rut, they would have missed out on God's best. God has a place of victory in store for every one of us, but it's up to us to find that place.

❧ Today's Prayer to *It's Your Time* ❧

Father, thank You for connecting my blessing to the right place.

❧ Today's Thought to *It's Your Time* ❧

I must stay on the course the Lord has set for me.

FIND PEACE IN YOUR SWEET SPOT

DAILY READING 5:13

SCRIPTURE READING TO *IT'S YOUR TIME*   DEUTERONOMY 33

Moses said this about the tribes of Joseph:
"May their land be blessed by the LORD
with the precious gift of dew from the heavens
and water from beneath the earth;
DEUTERONOMY 33:13 (NLT)

My FATHER USED TO SAY, "Learn to stay in your sweet spot." In baseball and golf, the sweet spot is the place on the bat or the golf club that gives you the most power when you hit the ball. My father applied it to a higher level. He was urging me to find the position in life designed for me by God. It, too, is the most powerful place, the location where you can most benefit from God's blessings in your life.

When you find your sweet spot, your place of blessing, you feel a deep sense of purpose and fulfillment. Search your heart and be sensitive to where it might be. It's not about financial rewards or material things, though they may come with the package. It's about receiving His full blessing.

You may be chasing a job, a relationship, or an opportunity. I encourage you to always seek to better your life but remember to stay in balance. There's more to life than money. A job relocation may include more money or benefits, but if the environment is not good, if you travel all the time and neglect your family, if you're surrounded by negative people, that may not be God's best place for you. Pay attention to your feelings. If you are unfulfilled, restless, and unsettled, the signs may be pointing to another location.

One of our church members, Hugh, just passed up a huge promotion from his employer. His company wanted him to move to another city. He prayed about it and didn't feel at peace with the offer. He didn't want to leave the church or his friends in Houston.

When Hugh turned down the promotion, his associates could not understand his decision. They thought he would jump at the opportunity for more money and a more powerful, prestigious position. But Hugh told me that deep down inside, he could not find comfort in moving away.

"Joel, do you think I'm making a mistake?" he asked.

I told Hugh that no matter how good the offer, if you don't have peace about it, it's not right for you. When I said that, a burden seemed to lift from his shoulders. He seemed so relieved. He accepted that he'd read the signs correctly. He felt at peace in his sweet spot.

I met a wonderful couple with several children from Bostwana, Africa. They lived in a little hut with no air-conditioning, no running water. It was hot. It was dirty. There was no television, no grocery stores or hospital. Yet every time I talked with this couple, they were as happy as can be.

I asked them if their lives were difficult. They looked at me in confusion and said, "Joel, we were wondering the same thing about you. How do you stay there in Houston with all that traffic and noise?" They told me that they were blessed and fulfilled right where they were—in their place of blessing.

You may be able to make more money somewhere else. Something may look more attractive to you. But when you're in God's perfect will, there is a peace and a fulfillment that money cannot buy.

In the first book of Kings, God commanded that Elijah's needs were to be supplied. But it was up to Elijah to reach the designated location. He had to be obedient. He could have said, "God, I'm comfortable where I am. I don't want to go down there."

If he'd done that, though, Elijah would have missed out. The ravens would have taken his provision down to the brook. God would have supplied his needs, but Elijah would not have been where he was supposed to be to receive the food.

How many of us have our blessings, our provision, ready for delivery but we're not in position to receive them? We didn't follow the still, small voice speaking to us. Maybe you are hanging around friends who are keeping you from receiving your blessings. You are not where you need to be.

Perhaps God opened up an opportunity, but you were not in position to receive it. You knew, deep inside, you should take it. But you were afraid to step forward or simply not where you needed to be at the time.

You need to put yourself in position to receive those blessings. I can't stand to think that God could be delivering favor, blessings, ideas, and creativity that I'm missing because I'm not where I'm supposed to be.

If you run from where God wants you to be, you may be missing out on His greatest gift. Be aware that God may be seeking to bless you in ways you never thought possible, ways beyond your comprehension.

❧ Today's Prayer to *It's Your Time* ❧

Father, thank You for putting me in place to receive Your blessings.

❧ Today's Thought to *It's Your Time* ❧

When I reach the place God intended me to be I will be even more blessed.

FIND A PLACE TO NOURISH YOUR GIFTS

DAILY READING 5:14

SCRIPTURE READING TO *IT'S YOUR TIME*   I KINGS 17:8–24

Then the LORD said to Elijah, "Go and live in the village of Zarephath, near the city of Sidon. I have instructed a widow there to feed you."

        I KINGS 17:8–9 (NLT)

SAMUEL AND HIS WIFE, SHARI, always wanted to start their own business, but they'd never done it because Samuel was making a good salary as a manager for a big company where he'd worked many years. He'd often talked to me about his desire to break out and start his own business, but he kept putting it off. He was afraid he might fail, afraid he didn't have what it would take.

Then one day Samuel heard me talking about listening to that "inner voice," stretching beyond the comfort zone, and taking calculated risks. He wrote me a letter and said I'd relit the fire that he'd allowed to die.

Samuel resigned from the big company and Shari quit her job, too. They pulled out all of their retirement money and invested in their own consulting business. They put themselves in position to receive God's greatest blessing.

Little by little, their business grew. God's favor increased. Samuel's former bosses had tried to talk him out of leaving. They said his new business would never make it. But they became his biggest clients. He tripled his income after a couple years. He and Shari have already built up more retirement money than they'd invested into their startup. They said, "Joel, we never dreamed we would see God's favor in the way we've seen it."

They found their place of blessing. They arrived at the brook where God commanded them to be blessed. Samuel and Shari told me that they struggled for a time, but because they knew they would reap the full rewards of their efforts, they were glad to keep working hard. God supernaturally put all the pieces into place for their benefit.

When you follow your instincts and pursue the life that fulfills you, you will never go wrong. Certainly, you have to be wise. Don't put your family's welfare at risk on a whim. Prepare yourself. Take care of your dependents. Act responsibly. But when you feel good about making the move, pray for God's guidance, look for His signs, and dare to take that step of faith. You don't want to reach the end of your life only to wonder what might have happened if you'd been willing to stretch yourself and reach for your dreams.

Elijah reached the brook. He was obedient, and God blessed him and met all of his needs. But one day, the brook dried up. The water quit flowing. The ravens quit coming. And so God told him, "Elijah, I want you to go to the city of Zarephath, for I have commanded a widow to take care of you."

Notice once again that God designated a specific place where Elijah's needs would be met. The key was that Elijah had to keep following the signs, getting to that place of blessing. Sometimes a brook will dry up. Sometimes God will push you into a new area. You have to be alert and willing to follow His directions.

When Elijah went to the brook, he was hiding from an enemy. Somebody had been chasing him. The enemy was from the city of Zarephath—exactly where God told him to go. Think about it: God could have sent Elijah anywhere, but He sent him to his enemy's hometown!

Sometimes God leads us to places that don't make sense to us. He has us leave a "safe" job to start a new, more fulfilling career. He breaks up a "comfortable" relationship and guides us to someone more loving, more caring, and more loyal.

✖ Today's Prayer to *It's Your Time* ✖

Father, thank You for guiding me to a place where I can nourish my gifts.

✖ Today's Thought to *It's Your Time* ✖

I will trust my instincts and when I feel good about making a move, I will pray for God's guidance, look for His signs, and dare to take that step of faith.

BELIEVE FOR A SUPERNATURAL YEAR

DAILY READING 5:15

SCRIPTURE READING TO *IT'S YOUR TIME*   PHILIPPIANS 4:10–20

And my God will meet all your needs according to his glorious riches in Christ Jesus.

PHILIPPIANS 4:19 (NIV)

A SALESMAN NAMED JAMIE KNOCKED on a door in Twin Falls, Idaho, hoping to sell a vacuum cleaner to the couple who lived there. Andi, the woman who answered the door, said they could not afford one because Paul was on disability with medical problems.

Paul's kidneys had been failing for more than a year, she explained. He was way down on a list of five hundred people awaiting a transplant. Part of the problem was that Paul had type O-positive blood, so he could get a kidney only from someone with the same blood type. None of their friends or family members was a match.

"I'm O-positive," the salesman said.

"Would you consider being tested to see if you could be a donor for Paul?" Andi asked.

Sensing her concern, Jamie said he'd think about it. He went to his car and prayed. Then he called his father, who is a doctor, and his wife. "I just felt this was something I was called to do," he told them.

A calm feeling came over Jamie. He hadn't even met Paul Sucher yet. He knew nothing about him other than the fact that they shared a blood type and Paul might die if he didn't find a donor.

Jamie knocked on the door again. This time, he wasn't selling. He was giving.

"I'll do whatever I can to help," he said.

Wouldn't you know it? Jamie and Paul were a perfect match. After months of testing and discussions with doctors, Jamie donated a kidney that saved Paul's life. Today, both men are healthy and strong.

Jamie never did sell that vacuum cleaner. But he is okay with that. "I had the opportunity to help someone and I had to take it," he said.

God knows what you need and He knows how to get it to you.

Paul Sucher never would have dreamed that a door-to-door salesman might offer to save his life. Who would ever think that God would send a vacuum salesman to donate a kidney?

God has you in the palm of His hand. He knows every need. He knows every struggle. He knows every dream, every desire. The good news is God has it all figured out. He's a supernatural God.

So often we limit our thinking. We think we'll never overcome our challenges or we'll never accomplish our dreams. We don't have the connections, the talent, or the funds.

But the problem is that we tend to look for answers only in the natural world. We have a limited perspective. We forget that God is a supernatural God. And just because we don't see a way doesn't mean that God doesn't have a way.

You may be impatient now: "Joel, if something doesn't happen soon, I won't get out of debt until I'm 122 years old."

I understand, but you should never rule out the power of *supernatural increase*. God can bring one opportunity across your path that will thrust you to a new level. He has explosive blessings that can blast you out of debt and into abundance.

A lady told me recently, "I don't think I'll ever get well. You should see what the medical report says about me."

That may be true according to the report from medical science, I told her. "But I have another report and it says you will live and not die. God is restoring health unto you."

The question is, whose report will you believe?

Today's Prayer to *It's Your Time*

Father, thank You for Your explosive blessings.

Today's Thought to *It's Your Time*

With men it may be impossible, but with God all things are possible.

GOD WILL OUTDO HIMSELF

DAILY READING 5:16

SCRIPTURE READING TO *IT'S YOUR TIME*   EPHESIANS 3:14–21

Now all glory to God, who is able, through his mighty power at work within us, to accomplish infinitely more than we might ask or think.

EPHESIANS 3:20 (NLT)

A FRIEND'S CHURCH WAS NEARLY done with a major building program, but they needed $2 million to complete the project. The pastor was encouraging the congregation, just challenging them to do their best. In passing he said, "If God were to give you the funds to pay off this project, how many of you would do it?" In other words, there's no pressure. You can't give if you don't have it. But if God were to supernaturally provide, would you make a commitment to give?

My friend Stefannie raised her hand when the pastor asked that question. She didn't have the money. But Stefannie said she was willing to give it to the church if somehow it came to her.

Well, several days later, Stefannie's friend Jessica called and told her that she'd been awarded millions from a major lawsuit settlement. She offered to give $2 million to Stefannie.

Stefannie was so excited. She was overjoyed.

"You are an answer to prayer," she said. "I know exactly what

I'll do with those funds. I'm donating it to my church to help finish that project."

A few days later, Jessica called Stefannie again.

"You know, I really feel like I'm supposed to give you two million dollars," she said. "So if you're giving those funds away, then I'm handing you an additional two million dollars for yourself."

It gets better. A few weeks after that, Jessica's attorney notified her that the judge had made another ruling in the same lawsuit.

"The other side has to pay penalties and interest," her lawyer said. "That means you will receive an additional four million dollars!"

My friend, that is *far and beyond* favor. That's God outdoing Himself. When it was all said and done, Stefannie was blessed. The church's building project was paid off. And Jessica didn't lose a penny.

But notice, it all began when Stefannie dared to believe for supernatural increase. When the pastor said, "If God gave it to you, would you give it?" she could have thought, *Aw, I don't need to raise my hand. I never get any good breaks. That will never happen for me.*

No, Stefannie was bold. As an act of faith, she said, "Lord, I believe." She was saying in effect, "I believe in supernatural increase. I know my job is not my source. God is my source. He owns it all."

⧉ Today's Prayer to *It's Your Time* ⧉

Father, I believe You can do infinitely more than I might ask.

⧉ Today's Thought to *It's Your Time* ⧉

Be bold and believe in supernatural increase.

AN HONORED GOD WILL FILL
YOUR HEART'S DESIRE

DAILY READING 5:17

Scripture Reading to *It's Your Time*   Genesis 18

Is anything too hard for the Lord? . . .
Genesis 18:14 (NLT)

When you put your faith out there, you allow God to show up and do amazing things in your life. My mother has always been a big believer in that. When I was a boy, Mom put it out there that she wanted a swimming pool. She was constantly talking to my father about it. But my dad was totally against having a pool.

"Dodie, swimming pools are too expensive, and they require too much upkeep," he said. "We don't have the time or the money. I'll get you something else but not a swimming pool."

Well, my father might as well have been talking to a tree. That did not faze my mother. She just went around the house saying, "One day we'll have a pool. It will be so fun. I can't wait to get out there in the water."

My dad would look at her like "Woman, what are you talking about? We are not putting in a swimming pool."

But month after month, even year after year, my mother kept thanking God for His goodness, thanking God that He was lining up the right people, the right opportunities.

She was believing for it. My dad was believing against it. But down in her heart she had a confidence, a knowing, that one day she would have that pool.

Every several weeks she would ask my father about it. "John, have you thought anymore about our swimming pool?"

"Dodie," he'd say, "I don't have to think anymore. I've told you a thousand times we are not putting in a swimming pool."

One day my father saw my mother in the backyard marking things off with a tape measure. He went out and said, "Dodie, what are you doing?"

"I'm just getting an idea where to put our new swimming pool," she said. My father thought, *This woman will not give up.*

About six months later a couple came to my father's church. They were strangers from another state. After the service they asked to speak to my parents.

"We build swimming pools," the man said. "We own a large company, and we flew all this way just to see if we could give you a swimming pool."

My dad nearly passed out.

My mother took the pool man by the arm and said, "We need to talk."

Needless to say, several months later we had a beautiful swimming pool in the ground, right where my mother had laid it out. I'll never forget the first time we swam in it. The kids, we were all so excited. We ran and jumped in. My mother got in, too.

A few minutes later, here comes my father in his swim trunks. His legs were so white they reflected the glory of God. He couldn't wait to jump in, he was so excited.

My mother looked at him and said, "John, don't even think about getting in my swimming pool."

What was that? Supernatural favor. God said if you will delight yourself in Him, He will give you the desires of your heart. That means if you'll keep God in first place, if you'll honor Him with your life, He'll cause people to want to be good to you. He'll cause you to be at the right place at the right time. His blessings will chase you down and overtake you.

Why don't you get out of your box and say, "God, I'm ready for some of these explosive blessings. I'm ready for Your far-and-beyond favor."

In Scriptures, God promised Sarah a child. At first she didn't believe it. She thought she was too old. I love what God said in Genesis 18:14: "Is anything too hard for the LORD?"

God says to each of us: "Is there anything too hard for Me?"

Do you think your dreams are too big for God to bring to pass? Do you think that a relationship is too far gone for God to restore? Do you think you have to live with that sickness the rest of your life?

No. Get a new vision today. Put on a new attitude. God is saying, "I am all-powerful. I can turn any situation around." It doesn't matter what it looks like in the natural. He is a supernatural God.

The Amplified Bible puts it this way: "Is anything too hard or too wonderful for the Lord?" Sometimes when we hear stories of supernatural blessings, we think, *That's just too good to be true. A friend gave you funds to pay off a building project? Somebody you didn't even know gave you a swimming pool?* Our down-to-earth minds say, *No way. That's impossible.*

But notice what kind of heavenly God we serve. He said, "Is there anything too wonderful for Me?" He's saying, "If you'll take the limits off Me, I'll amaze you with My goodness. I'll not only meet your needs, I'll take it one step further. I'll give you the desires of your heart."

One Bible translation calls these "the secret petitions of your heart." These are our hidden dreams, the secret desires and promises you haven't shared with anyone. They are just between you and God.

Know this today: God wants to bring your secret petitions to pass. Will you get a vision for it? Will you put your faith out there?

Sometimes we think, *Well, I couldn't believe for a swimming pool. That wouldn't be right.* Or *Joel, God's got bigger things to deal with than me getting this business off the ground, or taking this trip overseas to see my relatives. I can't bother God with that. That's not important enough.*

I believe it's just the opposite: God put the dream in your heart.

As a parent, I love to do good things for my children. I love to make their days special. Your Heavenly Father is longing to be good to you in the same way. He wants to amaze you with His goodness.

This is what my mother did with her swimming pool dream. She easily could have let my father talk her out of it. She could have come up with all the reasons why it was not workable and why she probably didn't deserve it. But she simply made a decision to stay in faith. She didn't try to figure it all out. She had the attitude, "Lord, I believe." She was saying, "God, I know You want to be good to me."

When you truly believe, it sets a series of events into motion. God gave that couple from out of state a desire to do something for my parents. Here they were hundreds of miles away minding their own business. All of a sudden they feel an urge to come to Houston. They have the idea, of all things, to give my parents a swimming pool. Why not just make a donation to the church, give them money, give them stock?

God wants to give you the desires of your heart. I believe even right now, because you're in faith, because you're saying, "Lord, I believe," God is arranging things in your favor. He is lining up the right people, the right opportunities.

In the coming days you will see supernatural increase, explosive blessings. God will give you the desires of your heart. That's just what happened to Sarah in the Scriptures. She eventually conceived even though she was way beyond the childbearing years. She had a son, Isaac. It was far-and-beyond favor, and she knew it. I love what she said.

"Who would have ever thought I could have a child at such an old age?"

In other words, she was so amazed, all she could say was, "Who would believe this would ever happen?" That's what God wants to do for every one of us.

☙ Today's Prayer to *It's Your Time* ☙

Father, thank You for blessing me in abundance.

☙ Today's Thought to *It's Your Time* ☙

God wants to give me some of these "Who would have thought?" blessings. God's dream is for me to say, "Who would have thought this would be my best year?"

GOD WANTS TO AMAZE YOU
WITH HIS GOODNESS

DAILY READING 5:18

SCRIPTURE READING TO *IT'S YOUR TIME*   PROVERBS 3

> *Trust in the LORD with all your heart*
> *And do not lean on your own understanding.*
> PROVERBS 3:5 (NAS)

YOU MIGHT AS WELL PREPARE. God has "who would have thought" blessings coming your way. You are headed for supernatural increase, supernatural healing, supernatural restoration.

Well, you say, "Joel, I don't see how that could happen for me. I don't see how I could ever get out of these problems. I don't see how I could ever be well."

Here's the key: You don't have to see how. That's not your job. Your job is to believe. God has all kinds of ways to bring your dreams to pass. He has ways you've never even thought of. Sometimes there is no logical solution. Sometimes there is no way out in the natural. If you constantly try to figure it, you will just get frustrated. Eventually, you'll get discouraged and just settle where you are. Again, understand this: Just because you don't see a way doesn't mean that God doesn't have a way.

Little Lindsey wanted a kitten. She kept asking her mother week after week for this kitten. But her mother didn't want any more pets around the house. She said no to her daughter's dream again and again. But this little girl was so determined she reminds me of my mother and her swimming pool dream.

Month after month Lindsey kept asking for that kitten. Finally, out of frustration, the mother said, "Listen, honey. If God gives you a kitten, I'll let you keep it. But we're not buying one."

Well, Lindsey didn't know any better. She went out in the backyard, got down on her knees, and said, "God, I'm asking You to please give me a kitten."

When she finished praying with the mother watching over her, all of a sudden out of nowhere a kitten comes flying out of the sky and lands a few feet away. The mother could not believe her eyes. She thought she was seeing things. There was no tree overhead. It looked like the kitten had fallen from the heavens.

Lindsey picked it up and said, "Look, Mommy. God gave me my kitten." The mother stood there dumbfounded, in disbelief.

Several months later she learned what had happened. The neighbors who lived behind her and a few houses down were trying to get this little kitten out of a tree, but the limb was too tall for the man to reach with his ladder. So this man tied a rope to the tree, and he hooked the rope to the back bumper of the car.

He started slowly pulling forward in the car to bend the tree over. Just when he got the tree bent low enough to reach the kitten, the rope slipped and the tree acted like a slingshot.

It slung that kitten nearly two hundred yards—three houses down—and it fell right at that little girl's feet. That man felt terrible. No one could find the kitten. He thought it was dead. He didn't know that he'd answered a little girl's prayer. God works in mysterious ways.

Now that little girl can say, "Who would have ever thought God would have rained down a kitten from the heavens?"

Is there anything too difficult for the Lord? Is there anything too wonderful for our God? He knows how to put you in the right place at the right time.

If you are single and looking for a relationship, God can bring the right person into your life. I wouldn't expect that person to drop out of the sky, though. If that happens, you better call the police.

But God can bring somebody great across your path. Don't doubt that. Remember the three simple words "Lord, I believe."

I met a couple at a bookstore in Manhattan not long ago. I was doing a book signing. They came up to the table and said this was their first wedding anniversary. Of course, I congratulated them. They were just beaming from ear to ear, so happy. They went on to say they had met at my book signing one year earlier in that same bookstore. They had never seen each other before. It just so happened they were standing in line next to each other. They visited for an hour or so. They ended up dating and eventually they got married.

Good things happen when you come to my book signings. I told that man, "You owe me a finder's fee."

She was a beautiful young lady. That young man can say, "Who would have thought I'd go to a book signing and come away with a beautiful wife?" Boy, that bookstore will be a popular place when word leaks about this!

My friend, God is in control of the universe. He is directing your steps, causing you to be in the right place at the right time. He knows what you need and He knows how to get it to you.

He can cause a salesman to knock at your door and give you a kidney. He can cause a friend to call you and pay off a mortgage. He can rain down a kitten from the skies.

I'm asking you today to release your faith for a supernatural year. You may have seen victories in your past, but what God wants to do in your future will supersede anything you've ever seen before. This is your year for far-and-beyond favor. This is your year for supernatural opportunities, supernatural connections.

You may not see how it can happen, but remember, God has a way. He not only wants to meet your needs. He wants to give you the desires of your heart.

And it's my prayer that you will get a revelation of how much your Heavenly Father is longing to be good to you. He even wants to give you the secret dreams of your heart. If you'll go out each day expecting to have a supernatural year, believing for supernatural favor, then you will see God show up and show out in amazing ways.

You will experience many "Who would have thought?" blessings—explosive blessings that will blast you to a whole new level. And when you look back, we can say, "This was not an average year, not a mediocre year. It was a supernatural year."

❧ Today's Prayer to *It's Your Time* ❧

Father, I know this is my year for supernatural connections. I thank You for directing my steps.

❧ Today's Thought to *It's Your Time* ❧

It's time to stretch! It's your time!